MW00563725

$100,000/Year and Freedom Too

Why Trucking might be the Life for You

Your Complete Guide to a Career in Over-the-Road (OTR) Truck Driving

By "Driver" Ed Wooderson

ISBN: **0997361301**
SBN-13: **978-0997361308**

Note to Readers

I have made an effort to explain every new word I have used and added an extensive glossary at the back so that you can look up any new word or term which you are unfamiliar with.

For any other words you are unfamiliar with go to freedictionary.org and they will access 21,589,880 words in 1061 dictionaries.

Katie, my 13-year-old granddaughter, is a keen student and googles every word she is not familiar with looking up 2-3 words a day. Having freedictionary.org as one of your icons and using it to help you with new words will let you, your kids and grandkids be great students.

Table of Contents

Forward

Who is this Book Written For?

When I first started writing this book, I thought my readers would be people looking for work as truck drivers, or those who currently drive a truck. My mission was to give the potential driver a Trucking 101 course explaining what over-the-road trucking was all about. I later realized a book about trucking could be of interest to a lot of people. Even people who may never be in a position to climb into a big rig.

As a teenager, I wanted to sail a small boat around the Pacific islands. I've read about it and dreamed about it for over 50 years. What I've realized is that we don't always live the dream, but it's important to have a dream.

In uncertain times it is nice to be able to envision a better life. Trucking can be that better life, which may happen in the future when the time is right.

If you are experiencing suffering, despair, or ruin, having a dream may stop you from being the victim of life. You may be able to stop worrying about things getting worse and realize that change for the better is possible.

When the right time comes, you can demand improvement

and have hope and realize that truck driving will help you accomplish your dreams.

No matter how crazy the kids are, how mean the boss is, or how hectic the commute is — it can all change. When the kids leave home you can say to hell with selfish bosses, lack of satisfaction at work, and you and your partner can drive off in a big rig.

A better life of personal responsibility, and the adventures you will encounter on the road can give you hope for a brighter future. One day you may take the plunge and drive a big rig, or maybe you might still be an  armchair truck driver just like I'm an armchair sailor: I read about boats but never got my feet wet. I accepted another challenge and sailed down the highway in a big rig.

Man's greatest virtue is that since time began he has dreamed of a better future. If man is fortunate, his dream will lead to production and results, but first he must have a dream. Hope for a better future can only occur when a better future can be envisioned.

I hope this book explains trucking well enough for you to see if trucking may be in your future.

The Trucking Industry's Nuts and Bolts

$100,000 More or Less per Year

You and your partner can make $100,000 a year without any investment, and accommodations are provided.

When two drivers, like a husband and wife, share the driving, this is called team driving. Two people drive the same truck — one sleeps and the other one drives. The free accommodation is the sleeper behind the seats. If you have family to spend your time-off with, you don't even have the expense of maintaining a home.

Teams can be paid about 50 cents per mile traveled, and this is split between the two drivers. A hard working team, employed by an efficient company, can run 5,000 miles to 6,000 miles per week and get paid $2,500 for the 5,000 miles or $3,000 for the 6,000 miles. You can see why top companies advertise that the team drivers who work for them earn $140,000 per year. The first year on the road, drivers may not make as much, which is why I use $100,000 more or less.

Have no one to team with? Become a trainer. Top trainers can make up over $100,000 per year. U.S. Xpress states a driver trainer can make over $110,00 a year.

Over-the-Road Truck Driving

Over-the-road (OTR) is when you drive a truck and don't get home every night. On some jobs, you get home every six to eight weeks and can be out longer — "out" for truck drivers means out on the road, away from home.

An irregular route carrier is one that cannot predict where a truck will be sent next. The unpredictability of where you will be next can be one of the biggest advantages of the job, but for a driver who wants to get home to his family it is the biggest drawback. If you run as a team with your partner or spouse, and getting home is not important to you, OTR irregular route truck driving has much in its favor. Every day is different. You meet new people all the time and see different things.

We seem to judge time by movement. If a lot has happened in the last few days, last weekend seems to be a long time ago. If nothing has happened in your life, then last weekend seems it was only yesterday. Spending a year truck driving seems like you've been doing it forever. Not only do you see many different things, but you get a lot of work done if you work for a company that does a good job of keeping you moving.

The hours are long, but you do seem to have more time. You may spend two or three hours chatting with other drivers before it's your turn to load, and then if you drive for 11 hours you've put in a long day.

Change is constantly occurring for the OTR driver. On one winter day, you may be sweating in the 90s in Miami. Three days later, you could be driving in the Midwest with the temperature below freezing. Then you may be nice and warm in Las Vegas, only to find yourself putting on chains in the snow as you come out of Reno, Nevada into California.

Before satellite radio, you could get bored driving between Dallas and El Paso along empty Texas roads. Satellite radio now offers a vast choice of entertainment, and you can always chat with another driver on the Citizens' Band Radio (CB).

If radio chatter bores you, it is good to have something to apply your mind to. You can listen to books on tapes, your favorite preacher or even immerse yourself in a new study. A songwriter can put together a tune. Some drivers try to solve the troubles of the world — myself, I find having time is no problem. I can always develop ideas for a book I intend to write. I don't know of any other job that pays $30 an hour, three times the minimum wages to work on your own projects. (The $30 an hour is 45 cents a mile, driving at 67 mph.) Usually, boredom is not a problem; there are too many things happening.

America has seen manufacturing jobs move overseas, and a lot of service jobs now have staff in India answering the phones.

However, truck driving will never be a job that can be done from another country. With the huge number of jobs that have moved overseas, truck driving may become a very attractive option, especially in areas where manufacturing plants have closed.

Even at current pay levels that are increasing by 8% to 12% annually, a decent living can be made in trucking. There is talk that pay rates must rise to attract the additional drivers needed to keep the economy moving. When this does happen, all drivers in the industry will benefit. But even without a big pay increase, good paying jobs are out there. This may not be apparent to the newly interested future truck driver. So this book will show the potential for someone, or a couple, who can set up a plan and stick to it.

Need to Save Some Money?

If you're a couple going on the road together, you're in a unique position to get a team driving job that pays very good money, plus you have a tax advantage of over $25,000 per year, as will be explained later.

While you're on the road, many of your regular living expenses can be eliminated or reduced dramatically. If you take time off at a family member's place, you don't have to pay rent on an apartment. If you own a home, you can rent it out and have the payments covered by the tenants.

You don't even need to own a car, especially if you work for a company that lets you keep your truck on your days off. This means no car payments, insurance, registration or maintenance. You may wish to rent a car occasionally to see the sights, but so what? It's still cheaper than maintaining your own vehicle.

If you really want to take a break from driving use Uber or Lyft, and really relax while enjoying a night out with a couple of drinks.

No more suits to buy or to get dry-cleaned for the office. Your company may supply a uniform. Fashion hosiery that every well-dressed lady must wear to work is no longer a weekly expense. No high heels are needed unless you are out having fun.

Adding to your clothing wardrobe while you're out on the road isn't feasible. There's simply no space for extra clothing in a truck. The clothes you do wear must be comfortable and serviceable. The endless clutter of material possessions that we spend so much money on is a thing of the past — there is just no room to store them.

The possessions that you do own are high-quality, serviceable items that you use on a regular basis — not like the things at home that you clean and dust but never use. It's not like you'll be denying yourself any toys to play with or exercise with. We seem to spend our time with small electronic devices. Laptops and tablets are being replaced by large screen smart phones. The trucking life will keep you in touch and pay you enough to keep your electronic devices upgraded and added to. You can buy a quality lens for your phone to take photos for Facebook while you travel.

You no longer need a fully equipped gym to stay healthy. Exercise equipment has become more portable. A lot of successful people need to stay fit while traveling for business. This need is met with the X-iser Portable Stepper. It stores in two cubic feet of space, folds to 20.5 inches by 13 inches by 4 inches and weighs only 40 pounds. http://www.xiser.com. Stepper exercises are one of the most effective cardio workouts you can have. It's based on the principle of stair climbing without the impact to the body of actually climbing stairs. I have used a stepper in the truck to keep fit while my wife drove. As you work on the stepper, you can work your arms with small weights. For arm exercises, you can use a bottle of water.

Eating out is no big thing — you do it every day when you are on the road. During your time off, it is a welcome change to help the family prepare a home-cooked meal for everyone to enjoy. Unless you want to go overseas, vacations are not something you want to spend money on. Who wants to travel, stay in motels, and visit distant family and friends when you've been getting paid all year to do just that? Even the trip to Vegas will have happened during work time.

Nobody comes knocking on your door for fund-raising or to sell things you don't need. There are no more phone calls asking for contributions to important causes you can't say no to.

If it is important for you to accumulate a certain amount of money to achieve your goals and purposes, I know of no better way to save money than truck driving as a team.

Taxes

"Per diem" is Latin for "per day." In the trucking industry, it has come to mean the daily amount of money you can spend each day for food that will be exempt from tax. Companies pay this money to drivers without having to deduct withholding taxes on the money involved. A special Internal Revenue Code Section 247(n)(3) allows truck drivers to deduct more of their meal expenses than any other taxpayer.

The daily allowance for food is $52.00 each day. Eighty percent is eligible to be tax deductible. This means $41.60 of what you spend every day you are on the road is money you don't pay tax on. No receipts are needed. Just keep a record of the number of days away from home. A husband and wife filing a joint return would be eligible for $41.60 each, a total of $83.20 each day both of you were on the road. If you were out for 300 days, the total amount of money you would not have to pay tax on would be about $25,000.

If you keep receipts, you can spend as much as you like on food and have 80 percent of the money you spend as a tax deduction. Check this out with your tax adviser.

You must, of course, be "away from home" to qualify for the tax advantage. If the IRS can prove that you have no place that actually is your home and that you live in your truck, you may lose this benefit. A tax adviser suggested to me that all OTR truck drivers should not use cash but should always pay with a check for their permanent residence. This is to establish a record that they have a place to live full time and don't always stay in their truck.

Of all things, the IRS allows you to always deduct your laundry expenses when you're on the road. It does make sense because if you were at home you'd just throw them into a machine, but when you're on the road you're limited to a truck stop. Those laundry machines eat more quarters than a Las Vegas slot machine. Hotel accommodations are deductible, so if you're stuck in Vegas for one or two days your hotel accommodations are deductible.

Some OTR truck drivers will move out of high income tax states to those that have no income tax. It actually makes sense to do so because if you're both on the road, you end up spending only a fraction of your time in your home state. Why pay tax to a state if you're not there to receive the benefits that are available to you as a resident of a high tax state? Check with your tax adviser on how your state income tax will affect you. If the money is not earned in the state, it may not be taxable. Before you change states, check with your tax expert.

Let's Crunch Some Numbers and Dream a Bit

Here is some number crunching of what you could make team driving with your spouse. Tax rates will vary from year to year and your tax situation so this is an estimation.

With pay rates increasing because of a shortage of drivers you can expect to make more than the figures I've shown.

Per diem is a tax-free allowance of $41.60 a day that a truck driver can spend on food.

Let's say in the first year you and your spouse only make:	$ 80,000
You live on the per diem. That is not taxable:	$ 25,000
You pay Federal Tax on:	$ 55,000
That Tax is:	$ 5,067
Amount left:	$ 49,933
Pay off bills and credit cards:	$ 25,000
Save:	$ 24,933

Year Two	
You make:	$100,000
You live on the tax free per diem	$ 25,000
Pay the IRS on:	$ 75,000
Tax:	$ 8,203
Save:	$ 66,797

Total Savings:		$ 91,730

Year Three

You Make:		$110.000
Live on Per Diem:		$ 25,000
Pay Tax on:		$ 85,000
Tax:		$ 10,172
Save:		$ 74,828
Total Savings:	$166,558	

Year Twelve:

Income:		$145,000
Save:		$ 99,379
Total Savings:	$1,043,804	

I have not included any state income tax because if you are serious about saving money, you will probably move to a state with no income tax. Of course, tax rates will probably change in the coming years, but this shows the potential of making money.

As I said, let's dream a bit. But you do need to check these figures out with your tax adviser. I haven't taxed the interest you earn on the money you save. If you set up a retirement with the help of a financial adviser, no tax will be payable on the interest generated by the savings account. Qualified retirement accounts pay no tax until after you retire and start to withdraw your savings. Seek help from someone who understands Individual Retirement Accounts (IRA).

By the same token, I haven't shown how much interest was added to the retirement account, which if invested wisely would, after some years, greatly add to your savings.

My calculations show if you earn 5 percent on your savings, non-taxable, it would be possible to save a million dollars in 10 years based on the previous figures.

Of course, none of this will happen. You will spend more than $25,000 a year. You will buy new personal vehicles perhaps put a child through college so they have no student loans. You may crave foreign travel or buy a home or pay off the house you have. Even if you are a new immigrant not used to the American lifestyle and can

15

really save money, you may send money to support your family back home.

During the Second World War, British Prime Minister Winston Churchill said you can trust Americans to do the right thing, after they have done everything else first. The right thing here is that Americans need to save some money to live comfortably in their retirement. Americans have tried everything else. They bought expensive vehicles with big loan payments. They let the credit card companies steal them blind. They refinanced their homes to pay off credit cards and spent money on expensive toys like RVs (recreational vehicles).

The right thing is to save some money, and if that is what you need to do, trucking can make it happen. If, like us, you actually enjoy the trucking lifestyle it is another advantage if you get paid well for doing what you enjoy.

I will end this section the way I started. I want you to dream a bit and see the potential of a husband and wife spending ten to twelve years as OTR truckers. Even if you only accomplish half of my not-entirely-impossible expectations, it'll make you so much better off financially in your sunset years.

How Drivers Are Paid

Drivers are mostly paid by the mile, so many cents for each mile you run, for example 46 cents a mile. Some companies pay more for shorter runs or pay different rates for running in different areas. For example, you would get more per mile running where there is traffic congestion compared with running west across New Mexico and Arizona.

Sometimes a retention bonus of a cent or two a mile is paid after you have been with the company for as little as six months. A safety bonus of a bit more per mile may also be paid if you meet the company's safety requirements.

Many companies pay more per mile for experienced drivers. For example, every year and up to seven years, a driver may earn an extra cent a mile. Therefore, a driver with seven years' experience will earn seven cents a mile more than someone just starting out.

Teams are paid more per mile than solo drivers. A sign-on bonus of up to $10,000 to $15,000 for teams has been paid by companies to attract experienced drivers.

Some companies will pay an annual cost of living bonus based on the previous year's earnings. If you've been employed for a certain amount of time, holiday pay and vacation pay may be given. Some companies even pay a longevity bonus, in addition to the extra types of pay outlined in the appendix.

Layover is when you're not going anywhere. It may be that you need to take a day off because you've done all the hours you're allowed by law and need to rest. It could also be that the load you were scheduled to pick up isn't ready, and you'll need to wait for it. Or it may be that no jobs are available until after the weekend, and you'll need to wait Friday, Saturday, and Sunday night before you can pick up a load on Monday.

Motel layover means the company will pay for a motel if you're laid over. This could be important if you're a team driver, especially if you aren't driving with your spouse. Some companies provide layover pay, usually so much per night and may not be paid for the first night.

Trucking companies can pay by the mile with no overtime pay because they're exempt from the laws that deal with minimum wages.

A union job pays by the hour. I've said very little about union jobs because you'll need experience for one of these jobs. The pay is good, and the benefits are excellent. A union job gives a guaranteed pension after a certain number of years. Because union jobs pay so well, they are hard to get. You will need to be well experienced before you can get one.

Keep union jobs in mind for the future, because you can get a local job and be home every night. Also as the baby boomers retire it will be easier to get a union job.

Is there any other way to make money apart from miles? Yes, there is. Almost every company will pay you a referral bonus if you encourage another driver to come and work for your company.

If you like talking to other drivers, or you or your spouse

have spent time in sales, and selling is in your DNA, the possibility for making extra money is good.

Some companies pay a $1,000 referral bonus for every experienced driver or owner-operator you recruit to work for them; e.g., $2,000 for a team. After a successful referral, you received $500 for each inexperienced driver or driving school graduate that you helped to get hired. My company will pay me $1,500 for a referral for a driver who is hired.

A $1,000 referral bonus for an experienced driver is paid by a lot of companies with one exception: Prime, Inc. also pays a mileage incentive based on the experience and classification of the driver you refer to them.

If you've worked in sales, you are aware that overrides can add up to big bucks if you and your recruits stay for the long haul (excuse the pun) with Prime. An example from Prime's website if you refer 8 teams and 5 solos you will earn approximately $72,000 (based on teams averaging 5000 miles and solos averaging 2500 miles).

The Lifestyle

How Do Drivers Live?

Most OTR drivers sleep in their sleepers behind the driver's seat. You can always check into a motel, but I have found that most drivers, who settle into the lifestyle, find it more convenient to just sleep in the truck rather than have the hassle of moving into a motel unless they are going to spend a night in a place like Las Vegas.

Summer, when the truck gets too hot for comfort, the engine is left idling all night to run the air-conditioning to keep cool. When it is cold, you need to keep the motor idling to stay warm. It's only very recently that truck engines were developed that will start and stop automatically to maintain correct temperature in the bunk area.

Sometimes the truck will have an auxiliary engine to provide heat or cooling without having to run the main engine. A heater that burns diesel can be installed in the truck to keep the sleeping driver warm on cold nights. Also there can be an air conditioner run on batteries that will keep the sleeper cold for eight hours. One of the advantages of team driving is that when you are running, one person sleeps and the other drives. The truck doesn't stop at night compared to a single driver. Thus the cab's temperature is maintained.

Drivers are typically assigned to a truck that is theirs, even if they are company drivers and the company owns the truck. On your day off you can drop the trailer and take the truck home. Or if you are away from home, and have a couple of days off, you can drive without the trailer to see the sights.

Who Supervises Drivers?

Most companies assign a fleet manager, also called a dispatcher, to individual drivers. The dispatcher is your communication link to the company while you are on the road. A dispatcher or fleet manager is the person responsible for dispatching and tracking your progress as you drive across the country. They get you loads and keep you moving. It's your dispatcher/manager who is responsible to get you home on a regular basis, and who handles any problems that arise.

Some companies have begun to supply mentors for new drivers. These mentors have been successful OTR drivers who provide advice and information to new drivers when needed.

Truck Stops

Truck drivers stay overnight at a truck stop or rest area. Truck stops are what they say they are — a place for a truck to stop and get fuel. The larger ones have a service bay for tires, oil changes, and small repairs.

Truck stops usually have a restaurant, or a fast food outlet, or both. Needed personal supplies or truck essentials can be purchased. The larger truck stops sell a variety of products. Non-truckers are amazed at what's available to support the truckers' every need.

Free showers are supplied if you purchase 50 gallons or more of diesel fuel. Towels and soap are provided to shower with, and the showers are cleaned by an attendant after use. They're not like the showers in recreational vehicle parks — truck stop showers are of a lot higher standard. Large truck stops even have hairdressers.

Truck stops have washers and dryers to clean your clothes. These laundry rooms are an interesting place to meet other drivers. This is especially true for you ladies. My wife got to know many wives who team drove, as she did our laundry. This gave her a chance to talk to other women, something she would not have been able to experience if it were not for her washing our clothes. It gave her a chance to get advice from more experienced drivers' wives when we were first on the road. She also picked up information on what to expect ahead, because she would meet people who were coming from the direction we were heading.

The driver parks his truck at the truck stop, eats in the

restaurant, and can watch a ball game with other drivers in the TV room or play video games. Drivers are seen working with their tablets and laptops hooked to the Internet Wi-Fi.

The driver returns to his truck to sleep and uses the truck stop facilities in the morning, before he continues his trip. Of course, a team can keep moving once the drivers have eaten and freshened up.

Immerse Yourself in the Lifestyle

Truck driving is more than a job; it's a lifestyle. Other professions may have similar demands. The military can dominate your whole time and attention, especially when you are deployed overseas and the family stays home. Medical training can consume every moment of your life, especially as an intern in a busy hospital, working 80 hours a week. Some sales jobs can be all consuming. The 2006 movie starring Will Smith, "The Pursuit of Happyness," showed how tough the pursuit is and how great the rewards can be.

Truck driving is the same. The lifestyle makes you part of a separate, hard-working group, but the interesting fact is that the job does not cut you off from society. (For instance, if you worked for the CIA you would be consumed by the lifestyle, but you could never socially discuss your job.)

Most people drive, so a truck driver can relate to most people he meets. A dentist was interested in my story of sitting in a truck at a warehouse where, after hearing a loud noise and some strong winds, a pale face appeared at my driver's window to ask if I was okay. When I asked what happened, the fellow said that a tornado had just torn off part of the building's roof. A dentist can only talk to other dentists about the details of root canals — but floods, fires, high winds, and icy bridges are real to almost anybody.

I have a friend in Los Angeles whose family lives in St. Louis. Whenever I meet her she says, "I still can't believe you leave Los Angeles late Friday night, unload and reload in St. Louis on Sunday, and are back in your own bed in Los Angeles, with the truck unloaded by Monday night."

OTR trucking does commit you to a lifestyle, but the good part of an OTR truck driving job is that you can share it with your spouse. You both have the same interest. Your goals and purposes are aligned. Your jobs keep you together and you stay married. Your jobs don't tear you apart.

What's more, you have a great view from your office window!

In Trucking, You Move On

Trucking is about getting the job done. At times mistakes will be made, but you don't end up living with them. You literally move on, because whatever mistake you make gets handled quickly. You don't live with unresolved issues. There is no unhandled paperwork left around for weeks. You start a job and finish it. There is no boss to pull you off what you are fully involved with to start something you think is unimportant.

You work with your dispatcher to get the job done. A dispatcher is responsible for getting loads for his drivers and supporting them in other ways. If things go wrong, the dispatcher will be in a position to handle the problem. Once you have established good rapport with your dispatcher, there is no one else who can give you orders out of the blue.

Especially if you're an irregular route driver, when there is conflict with a personality where you load or unload, there is every chance that you will never have to deal with that person again. You move on. You don't have to dread coming to work because someone is always on your back.

It is assumed you will drive responsibly and not get traffic violations or drive for more hours than the law allows. But even if you do, most companies have help available to handle the problems you may encounter.

Truck driving lets you do your job. You actually achieve something every day you drive the truck. You have a sense of accomplishment. You sleep well at night because you've worked hard and have gotten a result. You pick up a load, drive it to its destination and unload or drop the trailer. It's done. You get another job and complete that job. This makes you feel good about your work.

An Honest Life

Trucking is an honest life. You have to produce. You have to get things done. This is apparent if the truck is traveling at 70 miles per hour — you have to steer it. You can't delegate this job without getting out of the driver's seat. A trucker has to take personal responsibility. A truck driver has no choice but to make things happen and to make things go right.

A manager or worker in any other field can postpone, ignore or delegate anything he's not willing to handle himself. He can blame those he delegated when things go wrong. He can avoid personal responsibility.

In any other type of work, you can get involved in things that have no relationship to what you are trying to accomplish. Many unproductive hours can be spent on a whim of your own or some boss who believes thinking up new ideas is what he is paid for, when he's really paid for getting things done. With trucking this doesn't happen. When you drive from Los Angeles to San Francisco, you don't go via Las Vegas.

Trucking is a truthful life. When you are asked how long it is going to take to complete the job, you can't lie. It takes a known amount of time to drive a certain distance. In other types of work, if you are an optimist and are asked how long it will take to get something done, you will probably underestimate how much time is needed, and things will go wrong because you were too optimistic.

Sure, as a trucker you will run into traffic conditions and may not quite make it on time, but you can be honest about what happened.

As safety is uppermost in a trucking company's priorities, you can be honest and say the roads were too icy to drive safely so you pulled over. You don't have to feel guilty about not getting the shipment there on time. It is only occasionally, you will get delayed by weather, accidents or mechanical trouble, and when it does happen those waiting for you will be very happy you arrived safely.

If you play it straight and honest with your company, you will never have to feel bad about not doing your job properly. In fact, you can feel good about yourself because you pushed hard and did your best.

If honesty is the best policy and you play the game straight, trucking allows you to be honest with all those you come across. If honesty isn't your nature and you would detour to visit Niagara Falls, and then explain the delay by saying you had truck problems, don't become a truck driver. Stay with selling used cars or being a politician or a banker.

Crooks, con men and criminals need not apply. If you don't play the trucking game straight, it will eventually become apparent. The electronic records of where the truck traveled will show you went to Niagara Falls. Your lie will be found out, and your company will realize you can't be trusted and have to let you go.

If you are a man or woman of goodwill towards others and follow the golden rule of do unto others as you would have them do unto you, trucking is one of the best jobs I know. It lets you be totally honest, all the time, with the people you deal with. This allows you to feel good about yourself, your work, and your family.

If you live this lifestyle, and especially if you share it with your spouse, you can drive into a more fulfilling life along the road to happiness.

How Truck Driving May Align with Your Goals

Your goal may be to see the country instead of the inside of a cubicle. You may want to see new faces and meet new people. Sitting up high, seeing the world, beats just seeing coworkers in the same room.

A retired Navy veteran who had seen the entire world except

the USA, bought a truck and spent a number of years on the road while getting paid to see his own country. As he owned his own truck, he had the right to take loads only to places he wanted to see.

You can save money for that dream home — maybe even build it yourselves. If you take six months off work, your job will still be there if you want to go back to it. You can use your time out on the road for developing a business. You can check out what's done in other places, and also track down and go see all the suppliers you may end up dealing with.

Do you have a special hobby? Be at all the gun shows if you are a gun collector. If your hobby is buying and selling classic cars? You can get around the country and look at the cars you're interested in.

I once owned a 1963 Lincoln Continental Convertible. The type of car that President Kennedy was assassinated in. It's a four door convertible with the rear door hinged at the rear and open at the front and are known as "suicide doors".

In December 2015 I saw one advertised at about half the going price in Pennsylvania compared to what the price was in California. I had a team, Joe and Jesse driving near to where the car was with some hours to spare. I imagined, as the price was so low that that car was full of rust and was not a good purchase. Joe and Jesse were very knowledgeable about cars. Jesse is a trained mechanic. They found the Lincoln was in exceptional condition with no rust so I bought it for $14,500 and got it insured by a classic car company for $30,000. I was even in the position that my drivers could, if there were room in the trailer, pick the car up and return it to Los Angeles. Trucking made this possible.

Mad about race cars? Get enough experience as a truck driver, and then start looking for a job that hauls the racing teams' cars and equipment.

If you would really rather be driving coaches full of rich tourists because you've heard the tips are good — no problem. Get some experience driving a truck and then talk to every coach driver you meet at truck stops to find out about hauling tourists. You might even wind up driving a million-dollar motor home for a rock or country music star on a concert tour.

Ladies, are you tired of wearing a false smile, worrying about your wardrobe, making up your face, grooming yourself perfectly, and driving a long commute to work? Maybe you just want to say "to hell" with sales, schedules, selfish bosses, and you and your man drive off into the sunset as team drivers.

Even lawyers have been known to sell their practices to do something more positive — team drive with their wives.

You Will Meet Some Great People

Truck driving has a unique appeal about it. The people you work with are there to help you. I've met some really good people who bent over backwards to help me get my truck loaded or unloaded.

A majority of truckers have a great attitude toward helping on and off the road, as demonstrated through Trucker Buddy. A truck driver can adopt a school classroom and give the kids the experience of inspecting his truck whenever he visits the school. The Trucker Buddy driver sends post cards from his travels and makes the truck driving experience real for school kids.

The industry seems to attract people of good will — maybe because there is no competition to get promoted or fight over commissions. It's good to work with helpful, unselfish people.

Like Gary, who has jumped on and off so many forklifts and trucks that he's worn his hip out. Now, with a replacement hip, he stays happy as he tries to wear out his other hip. Steve cares for a wife whose medical problems are daunting, but he's still cheerful as he loads me at 2:00 a.m. Kurt stays late with no overtime to get us unloaded.

These are just a few of the warehouse personnel I've met. As new drivers, my wife and I needed all the help we could get. It was straight out of school with a trip to New York in winter, but there was always a driver there to help us when we needed help. Thanks, guys. You helped keep us in the industry and made this book possible.

You all meant it when you said, "Have a good trip." And yes, it's been a great trip.

Seventeen Weeks of Vacation Each Year

This is definitely not the American way. How does it work?

It's where three drivers or three teams share two trucks. The driver or team is out for two weeks, and then has a full week as home time. As a result, you have 17 weeks at home each year.

You will earn about 15 percent less than being a regular driver having exclusive use of a truck. This brings up the sore point of "slip seating," where one truck is shared by more than one driver, and one driver slips out of the seat and the other slips in. There can be problems if the truck is not left tidy for the next driver. The three drivers or teams must live reasonably close to each other so the switch can be made.

The advantage of three drivers/two trucks is that you know exactly when you will be off in the future. You can plan ahead to efficiently utilize your time off.

This is a good option to have available in the future after you've visited Graceland, Niagara Falls, etc. and the wanderlust has been satisfied. Or if some time in the future you need to spend time at home with your grandchildren.

It's also an option you should have available if you start trucking because of money problems. Once you've handled your bills and have a comfortable amount of money saved, you'll have the option of having more time off to catch fish or play golf.

Even with 17 weeks off, this is considered a full-time job, so all of the other benefits apply.

I believe that, to make this work, you will probably need to drive for a large company that has other drivers living nearby.

Schneider International's website mentions 17 weeks vacation so talk to Schneider.

After Over-the-Road Driving

After you have spent a few successful years on the road, what happens if your family responsibilities are such that you have to be home more often? Of course, you can get a local driving job and be home most nights and weekends.

Unless it's a union job, you will take a substantial drop in income. But if you are an experienced OTR driver, with a clean driving record, as the baby boomers retire there will be openings for well-paying union jobs.

If you don't want to drive, you can get a job as a dispatcher. Who better to work in management positions in the transport industry than truck drivers who actually know what being on the road is all about? Some drivers, while on the road, take online management courses to qualify for a future management position.

Some companies are providing mentors especially for team drivers. These mentors are or have been in top earning teams and their hands-on experience puts them in a position to develop the abilities of new teams. After OTR driving, you could become team mentors for your company, or another company that supports mentoring.

If you're team drivers, running for an efficient company, you'll make excellent money and be in a position to buy a piece of property. If you know where you want to settle once you are off the road, why not buy a duplex or a triplex, or even a large income property that can be rented out to pay the mortgage.

In 1998, we bought a house with two attached apartments. It has worked out very well for us. We have lived in one of the apartments and rented out the rest. With current real estate prices and drivers making good money, this will again be possible in the future.

If you are a go-getter and really want your own business maybe the best option is to keep the truck but get out of the driver's seat and employ drivers to work for you.

To make this really work you must stop driving and manage your business so you have the time and energy to hire and train new drivers. Too often I have seen a driver get a second truck and try to manage his business while he is still driving his first truck.

George has been with the company I'm with for as long as me. He has two team runs but has kept driving until he ended up in hospital needing serious heart surgery.

I believe if George had gotten out of the truck and only driven like I do when the best planning breaks down and it's an emergency then things would be better for him. It is human nature to take the easy way out and getting in the driver's seat is easier than hiring another driver and going through all the problems of training them well enough to do the job. If George had gotten out of the driver's seat and used all his energy to increase his fleet, he might have been under less stress and maybe his medical problems would not have been so severe.

Trucking is a good business. If in the future, you will need to be home more often seriously consider how you can stop driving and start managing.

Of course management is a skill in itself. Maybe as you drive and take online management courses so in the future you will have the business skills to manage your own trucking company. Or my next book needs to be how to manage a small transport company.

Who Should Become Truck Drivers?

Love to Drive?

When I was out driving with one of my drivers, Ron, I mentioned that I hate driving my car. His unexpected response was that he also hated driving his car. After all, it was much easier to drive a truck.

For one thing, Ron emphatically explained, he doesn't sit high up like in a truck and can't see over the cars in front of him. He said that driving a car around town was totally different than running the open road at highway speeds.

A truck is fun to drive because of the great view and the large mirrors. They make the driver feel in control. Especially, driving on the open road with other trucks and drivers helping one another.

Trucks have two switches on the steering wheel – one is to turn the headlights off at night for a moment to tell another truck driver who is passing that he can safely pull back into the outside lane. The other switch turns off the rear marker lights to thank the driver for indicating it is safe to pull back in. In daylight, the switches flash the headlights or rear marker lights.

When driving the interstates, especially at night, there are a lot of big rigs on the road. It is good to know these are driven by well-trained professional drivers.

I recently talked to one driver who lives in Canada. During the cold months, he takes time off to tow his Harley behind his van and goes to Florida to participate in motorcycle events.

His statement was simple: "I love to drive."

It's good to do something you love and if it is driving, why not become an OTR truck driver and earn an income for what you love to do.

Single Drivers

Traditionally, companies have employed single drivers. A lot of companies, because they run relatively short distances, still use single drivers. Many of these single OTR drivers have a pet, a dog or a cat, to keep them company.

If you haven't got a spouse to run with, you can become a trainer. Trainers make good pay. Swift Transportation calls their trainers mentors and pays the mentors up to $90,000 a year. (See the later chapter on Trainers.)

Spouse Rider Program

Most companies will allow a spouse to accompany the driver without the spouse being licensed to drive a big rig. This handles the problem of the husband and wife being separated while the driver is at work. The spouse is always there for companionship for the driver. The spouse can also help the driver with the paperwork and customer relations.

An OTR driver can be out on the road, living in the truck, for weeks at a time. For a single person or a married couple, no home needs to be established; therefore, expenses can be kept low and money can be saved. If you, as a couple, would like to travel together throughout North America but one of you is not capable or doesn't want to drive a big truck, don't give up.

First look into driving a smaller expediter truck. Expediter trucks have teams to get a small load quickly to its destination. This truck is no bigger than a motor home, and a big rig license is not required. This is fully explained later in the book.

If one of you just doesn't want to drive, look into moving household furniture. The non-driver can keep busy with the extensive paperwork that is required. This is also covered later in the book.

Some companies pay good money if a driver encourages another driver, from a different company, to switch jobs and drive for his company. A non-driving spouse can earn extra money talking to other drivers about the advantage of working with their company. This gives non-drivers an interest and lets them earn extra money. This is covered in more detail in the chapter on how drivers are paid.

Some contracts let the driver find his own loads. These loads usually pay a percentage of the money paid by the shipper for moving the freight. This can add more profit for the driver if he really spends time to find good paying loads. The driver's spouse can spend the time needed searching for good paying loads. The spouse can be in the truck with the driver or at home securing loads.

Women in Trucking

Let's face it. Until recently, trucking has always been a man's world. With the advent of team driving, wives started driving with their husbands, and women became part of the long-haul trucking scene. Women teamed with other women as well, and more women were trained as solo drivers.

An association has been formed to support women drivers. Ladies, you can become a member of Women in Trucking — WIT. One of the goals of WIT is to bring women and men in the trucking industry together to encourage and support more of their female peers to consider trucking as a career opportunity.

Ellen Voie, founder of Women in Trucking association said in December 2015, "When you work in a male dominated profession you make typically more money than when you work in a female dominated profession. So as a truck driver you make the same amount of money as your male peers, because you either get paid by the mile or as a percentage of the load. So gender is not an issue for pay in truck industry for drivers."

At present 6% of truck drivers are women but there is a concerted effort to get more women into big rigs. More women are teaming up with their husbands especially empty nesters or increasingly millennial couples that may be looking to save some money before they settle down to start a family.

To make this happen companies are upgrading their fleets with easier to drive automatic transmissions. Schneider International has announced all trucks will have automatic transmission by 2019. Also the drivers' cabs are being designed to accommodate all sizes including small women.

Werner Enterprises says a driver can make $50,000 to $60,000 in the first year, and Werner has found that women outperform men in several key economic ways. "Our female drivers have about a 25% lower accident cost", said Derek Leathers, President and Chief Operating Officer at Werner. "They're having smaller accidents. They're not having the big ones… maybe the attention to detail is a little better, maybe the focus or maybe just the concern is something they bring to the party that just makes them better drivers."

Ellen Voie said that's the feedback from other companies as well "What carriers are telling me is that they want more female drivers for the safety issue and …. women are often better with customers, paperwork, better with equipment and easier to train."

Of my 10 drivers I'm blessed to have Susan so 10% are female drivers. The warehouse we load and unload at are usually all male so Susan has a charmed life because the guys loading or unloading her truck bend over backward to help her.

WIT has a newsletter where members can read about other women who have interesting stories to tell, and see what their sponsors have to offer them. WIT also holds receptions at industry events providing a way for members and their sponsors to socialize. This can also be done through the bulletin board on the WIT Web site. Members can ask questions, introduce themselves, and give their input to one another.

WIT also links members to carriers who are sensitive to the issues women face on the road. Now it is possible to discern which companies support and encourage the women they hire. Before WIT, this could only be gained by referrals and instinct, such as; ladies should not drive for the "Bad Boys" trucking company. Now WIT supplies you the information you need to get started and continue a career in trucking.

Look for Women in Trucking at www.womenintrucking.org

Team Drivers

On longer distances it is more economical to have a truck driven almost continuously by two drivers to keep it moving. This saves on the cost of idling overnight when the truck is stopped. Team drivers make better utilization of the truck. A team can do almost twice the work of a solo driver.

Transport companies have found that drivers are happier if their spouses are with them. Husband and wife driving teams have fewer accidents and claims for damaged freight than single drivers.

Husband-and-wife teams are willing to stay out longer and cover a far greater distance than single drivers. Some companies expect their teams to be out for a month, or drive 20,000 miles before they get a few days at home. A single driver would only do 10,000 to 12,000 miles in a good month.

Team drivers, also called Teams are therefore paid more per mile than single drivers — usually five cents to six cents per mile extra when you run as a team. Drivers other than married couples are hooking up to earn the higher wages that are paid for team driving.

The "sign-on" bonus is higher for teams compared with single drivers. Teams can be offered a sign on bonus up to $15,000 when teams are really needed. A "sign-on" bonus is paid to attract experienced drivers; it is a sum of money paid after some months of employment.

I have always been a team driver, with either my wife or other drivers. It's surprising how far you can go with two drivers. Going 2,500 miles in two days is not unusual.

Werner Enterprises expects their teams to run 1,000 miles per day. Schneider International says their teams average 5,000 to 6,000 miles per week because they have priority freight selection and dispatch. In some companies, teams get preferential treatment over solo drivers on freight selection and dispatch, so the team spends less time loading and unloading, and more time driving.

If you decide to run as a team, only work for a company where the teams are managed separately from the solo fleet; otherwise, your dispatcher will want you to take loads that don't need a team, and you will not get the miles.

Also check out the average length of the team runs. The longer the run, the more miles you will get and the more money you will earn. A long run lets you arrange your sleep schedule better so you don't get so tired.

If possible, get a team job that is "drop and hook" and the terminals where you change trailers are open 24 hours a day, seven days a week. Drop and hook is where you change trailers without having to unload or reload. Drop one trailer and hook onto another pre-loaded trailer, and you're on your way. You don't want to be stuck with no load on Friday night, waiting for a business to open on Monday.

My wife and I started trucking as a team. I didn't know, when we were first hired, how valuable we would be to a trucking firm. A husband-and-wife team who is willing to run hard and stay out for extended times will always be in demand.

In our early 50s, with an empty nest, we could have had any team-driving job we wanted. As we didn't know this, we settled on a company that didn't utilize its teams to the fullest. Sure, we used to get them out of many mishaps when the load wasn't going to get there on time. We would even swap trailers with a solo driver in the dark of night at some truck stop to get the freight to its destination on time. But we should have worked for a company that specialized in teams and kept us busy.

Team drivers are very much in demand. For a husband and wife, it is a great way to see the country and save a large percentage of your pay.

Trainers

In an effort to make new drivers safe, many companies use trainers. Once a new driver has a CDL (commercial driver's license), he teams with an experienced driver, and they drive together for some weeks.

Want to team drive and have no other half? Become a trainer. Some companies will employ trainers with as little as six months' experience.

Being a trainer has many advantages. You get paid higher because of being part of a team. Your pay is also increased because you are training someone else. Werner Enterprises' potential earnings for a trainer are $65,000 to $100,000. Prime Inc.'s Web site states, "$2,800 maximum earnings per apprentice based on non-spouse training." It seems that this is the potential earnings for having a student run with you for a few weeks. If you do a good job, and the student stays with Prime for a year, the reward can be as high as $2,800. Swift Transportation gives an example of a trainer's yearly pay, with six years' experience, driving 3,600 miles a week. I quote: "Annual pay — $87,325 + $11,520 bonus potential — approximately $98, 845." US Xpress says a driver trainer can make over $110,000 per year.

As a trainer, you are not alone. You have someone to eat with. Just when you've run out of experiences to talk about, you get another student to train. Usually your student becomes a friend, but in the rare case where you might not get along with your student, you are only stuck with him for a few weeks, and you'll soon get a new student that you can relax with and enjoy your time together.

It's not a perfect system, because training is a skill in its own right. Some people are just not patient enough to teach.

I was a driving instructor in New Zealand, teaching driver's education before I became a truck driver. I taught many older people to drive who had attempted to learn to drive in England, where the test is designed to have the driver fail. When they arrived in New Zealand, they again got professional driving instruction but never got confident enough to even try to take the test.

I learned from those failed students how to teach driving. They taught me what driving instructors did that got in the way of the student learning quickly. Some instructors have learned how to teach, but others don't have a clue and actually do damage.

From talking to truck drivers who have been with trainers, it's the same situation. Some trainers yell and scream for no reason. Others have learned to stay calm. One driver I employed had left the industry because his trainer made him feel that he could never drive a truck. I got him driving confidently.

My book *How to Teach Your Baby and Teen to Drive* (which

can be purchased from Amazon) teaches adults how to teach their children to read the road and predict what other drivers will do. This should be taught to a teenager in the passenger seat of a car before he is old enough to get a license. I've used the material in the book to make confident truck drivers.

My book also explains how to teach someone to drive a car once they have a learner's permit. This book can be used by a trainer so he knows how to help the inexperienced truck driver learn quickly.

If you would like to be a trainer but are not sure how to go about it, buy my book. It should answer your questions and make it possible for you to be a successful trainer. Even if you intend to just run with your spouse who needs to become a bit more confident, this book will show you how to help her.

My wife was pulled over for speeding. The cop didn't give her a ticket because he said that she wasn't the driver. He was so sure a man was driving — after all, a woman couldn't drive as well as my wife was driving. I had applied what I had written to teaching my wife to keep the truck perfectly centered between the lanes. This is what must have impressed the cop.

Sometimes the best teacher is someone who has recently been taught the subject. This is because how he learned to do it as a student is still fresh in his mind. I employed Ron when he had only eighteen months' experience. He had been offered a position as trainer with his previous company and had turned it down because he considered he was still learning, and without years and years of experience, thought he shouldn't be a trainer. It was true that he was still learning, but he didn't realize that he also remembered how he was taught.

I put an inexperienced driver on the road with Ron. This driver was having trouble shifting gears. Ron quickly resolved the new driver's shifting problem, while the previous driver he teamed with, who had many years of experience, had been unable to help. That inexperienced driver told me that Ron has helped him with many little things that he didn't know he could improve.

The ideal teaching situation is when someone who has just learned the skill teaches another. Of course, the new teacher will need some help from an experienced instructor who knows all the tricks of the trade. When the student stumbles and the new, inexperienced teacher doesn't know how to handle it because it is something he has never encountered, a phone call to the lead trainer should sort it out.

I have on my Web site an instruction guide that covers all the points of instructing someone to drive a car. If the guide makes sense to you, buy the book. It fully explains all the points in the instruction guide, and you can apply them to driving a truck. You could be on your way to supplementing your new career as a truck driver with a training position.

Empty Nesters

The nest is empty, the last of the children just headed away to college. Life no longer runs on the fast lane. It's just the two of you. After years of hectic activity, of having a house full of kids and their friends, the biggest event of the week is now a call from one of those children who used to fill your life with confusion.

If you should be empty nesters but a grown child is too used to being looked after by Mom and Dad, why don't you be the ones who sneak out for a new adventure?

Your jobs are on hold. You can't see any chance of advancement. Why not take a leave for a year or two and become an over-the-road truck driver, and you'll get to see your kids as you drive around the country? They won't need you to mind the grandchildren for a few more years, and right now you have a golden opportunity to see the sights and get things happening in your life.

My wife and I were empty nesters when we trained as truck drivers. Trucking companies are putting out the welcome mat for mature drivers for some very good reasons. They have found that mature workers become safe and responsible truck drivers. Because of that maturity, they have enough experience to know what they are capable of and, as a result, they stay safe on the road.

One third of Schneider International drivers are over 50 years of age. In November 2005, Schneider joined the American

Association of Retired Persons' (AARP) "featured employer" list of 23 U.S. companies. These companies were selected based on their hiring practices, their benefits, and opportunities for mature workers. Schneider went from 15 percent of new hires over the age of 50, to 48 percent of their new people.

Use Trucking to Move your Kids into the Middle Class

John drove for me as a team driver. He has made a serious attempt to raise his children into the middle class. One son is an electrical engineer, a daughter is a nurse and in one year his youngest daughter will be a medical doctor. John tells me that truck driving has moved all his kids into comfortable jobs because truck driving has made enough money to put all his kids through college without student loans.

As a truck driver while not spending too much on himself he has paid $40,000 per year towards his youngest daughter's medical training who will soon herself be earning good money as a doctor.

America has always held up the hope that working class families can move their children up into the middle class through higher education. Student loans now appear to trap those who do make it as they have the burden of student debt for many difficult years.

John used trucking to help his kids to a better life without student loans. An empty nest married couple could easily send a child through college without student loans and propel their kids into well-paying careers.

Retired and Bored

I've met many active retired people on the road living in large motor homes. If travel is your thing, why not let someone else pay for the diesel fuel? Become part of a group by working for a transport company. You don't have to run big miles — only take a job if you are ready to move on. This is explained under "non-forced dispatch" later in the book.

Let's face it, people are living longer. If you have taken care of your health, the prospect of living a long, active life is good.

Norman Borlaug, the scientist behind the Green Revolution who developed more productive crops that increased the world's food supply, was asked when he was 70 to take on a project in Africa. He said, "No, I'm too old." The Japanese man who wanted him to go to Africa called back the next day and said, "I'm 86 years old, we need to start tomorrow." Norman Borlaug died in 2009 at 95, but during his last 25 years he increased Ethiopia's crop production by 30 percent. Not bad for a man who thought he was too old at 70.

I was also struck by a 114-year-old woman when the interviewer asked, "Have you had a good life?" Her answer surprised me when she responded with, "I don't remember, it was so long ago."

Modern research has shown a long, active life is possible if new challenges have to be dealt with. The challenge has to be a vocation, not just a hobby. Playing a round of golf every day isn't a big enough challenge. Maybe the hobby of seeing the country in an RV needs to be turned into a vocation of driving a truck.

If the seed expert can take on a project in Africa when he was 70, even though he thought he was too old to start a new project, surely at a bit younger age you can start a new career — trucking.

The challenge of driving to new places and doing new things will give you a whole busy life. If you ever get to 114 and someone asks you, "Did you have a good life?" You can answer, "Yes, I had several good lives, but the most interesting and exciting was satisfying the wanderlust I had as a youngster and having the whole 48 states to drive over." Sure beats the hell out of sitting on the couch where the biggest challenge is looking for the TV remote.

I've change my name from Eddie to Ed to become Driver Ed and start a new life as a writer. A friend's wife after 75 years moved into a new town and changed her name from Alice to Alison. A new vocation and even a new name make sense to me as we create new challenges later in life.

With the possibility of retirement lasting 40 years, even if it is not an economic necessity it makes good sense to start a new vocation as, or before, you get to the traditional retirement age of 65.

To be a real challenge to keep you young, the challenge needs to be something new. A chef starting his own cake shop is not new, it's still cooking and that's not a new challenge.

Many people spend their lives working in front of a computer screen without any real adventure. The adventure of distant places and new faces with the personal responsibility of a powerful big rig would be a challenge that would add to your productive years and, if needed, add to your economic security.

Should you lack income for retirement, a few years on the road could change all that. Check with your doctor to see if you meet the requirements to pass a medical test to obtain a commercial motor vehicle license. If your health is good, a few years on the road could let you live more comfortably in your old age. If you are over 65, Medicare will take care of the major part of your medical needs. This should make you more attractive to hire, because the company you work for will not have to pay the high cost of health care.

Don't Know Where You Want to Live Once Retired?

Many people in this situation retire, put their belongings in storage and spend a couple of years on the road in an RV looking for the perfect retirement spot.

My wife and I, while not at retirement age, were in a similar situation. We immigrated to the USA and quickly wanted to get out of Los Angeles. While truck driving around the 48 states, we checked out each location that suited our needs. We found our perfect spot at Daytona Beach, Florida.

We were laid over in Florida during the July 4th weekend and, quite by chance, again on Thanksgiving weekend. We saw Daytona Beach at two different times of the year and liked the music and action. I could take a walk at midnight and still have people around me. We also checked out New Smyrna Beach, a little further south of Daytona, and if we had been looking for a quiet seaside resort it would have been perfect. Truck driving gave us this opportunity.

Our daughter took us at our word and also moved from California to Florida. She bought a large fixer-upper home eight minutes' walk from the beach. Later we followed our daughter back to California to be with our grandchildren.

If you haven't yet found the place you want to call home in your later years, truck driving will get you there. Once you think you have found the spot you want, you can check it out at different times of the year. Make sure you look it over when the weather is at its worst, as well as on a perfect day. So many people retire to a place they once saw while it was at its best on vacation but later move away from it because their expectations were too high.

Of course you can do this in an RV, but why not let someone else pay for the diesel? Spend some time truck driving and get paid to find the perfect spot.

Want Your Own Home but Can't Afford Big City Prices?

If you want more bang for your buck, over-the-road truck driving allows you to buy a home away from expensive cities. After all, you don't have to drive to work and back every day. The freeway commute doesn't have to be a part of your life five days a week. Truck drivers have been known to sell their homes in expensive areas and relocate to places far away from the cities. When you go to work and are going to be out for a while, a two-hour drive is not a hardship compared with two hours commuting each day.

Werner Enterprises states, "Thanks to our many divisions and diverse operations, our drivers may live in any area of the country they prefer."

CRST Malone, who call themselves America's largest team carrier, states they have dedicated runs available in Atlanta, Memphis, Fort Worth, Seattle, Portland, San Francisco, Dallas and

Chicago. So if, for example, you were to work for CRST Malone and wanted to have a dedicated run, you could establish your home in an area where it would be possible to have a dedicated run in the future.

Watkins Shepard hires van drivers who live a reasonable distance from various company terminals.

Many drivers have settled in picturesque areas of the country and away from the large, polluted cities. Some have taken time off work to build their own log cabins or conventional homes. Some have gotten out of the warmer areas and bought or built a home where they can enjoy all of the seasons, including, with luck, a white Christmas. Truck driving makes this all possible.

Some drivers move close to the head office so, if they choose to get off the road at some point in the future, they can stay with the same company and get a desk job. Maybe they'll become a dispatcher, or if the company has a CDL training program, help others to become professional truck drivers.

Headquarters for trucking companies are not downtown. They have to have truck access, so getting a job in the head office won't usually involve a long commute into a city.

Some drivers just stay on the road like we did, until they see where the kids settle down, and then move to be where their kids are so they will be closer to the grandchildren.

Moving isn't usually a problem. If I was not in a position to move my own possessions as part of a load I was transporting, my company makes shipments for me for just $150.

As a truck driver your horizons expand. It gives you plenty of opportunities to have your dream home, by a river or a lake, or somewhere you can dirt-bike, hunt, or fish. You can probably even find a place where green fees are affordable and improve your golf handicap.

Millennials

OOIDA (Owner-Operators Independent Drivers Association) fights for the rights of all professional truckers; owner-operators, company drivers and small fleet owners. If you intend to stay with trucking, you should join OOIDA.

Land Line, the official publication of OOIDA, has an interesting article in its March/April 2016 issue entitled "Faces of the Future" and I quote "Derailed by recession, a new generation of drivers – resilient, results orientated young people are finding a home in trucking." OOIDA has almost 20,000 members who are 35 years or younger.

It seems that trucking may once again be appealing to its traditional recruiting pool. It used to be young people who were dissatisfied with a number of low paying jobs who would get into trucking and stay for 30 to 40 years. Recently companies have been hiring older drivers but it seems that millennials are looking at the advantages of trucking to achieve their American dream.

While on the road millennials can take advantage of all the new technology they are familiar with to stay in touch. They can apply the new technology to making their truck business more productive. Their energy and drive will make it possible for these young people to go from company driver to owning their own truck, then to becoming a fleet owner with more than one truck.

I got into trucking in my 50s as an empty nester and without a plan I have managed to stumble my way into becoming a fleet owner with seven big rigs. My income tax returns state my corporation turned over one and a half million dollars in 2015.

If I had been 25 years younger when my wife and I got into trucking and we had had a plan to expand (any plan even if it wasn't perfect) it makes me wonder what the potential might have been. We were new immigrants from New Zealand when we arrived in America in 1994. I had a health problem (since resolved) and I didn't have the energy to move into sales where my background was so I decided to sit and drive a truck until something better showed up.

Like most truck drivers we fell into the trap that the next load is important but no long term future plans are evolved. Whatever plans we had included looking for some other business to get into without realizing that trucking had so much potential for us to flourish and prosper. Somehow it worked out well for us. We now have a stable business, own property and even bought a toy to play with, my 1966 Lincoln Convertible.

I enjoy working with and helping my drivers and now with my daughter Shelley doing the boring paperwork I keep an interest as I celebrate my 75th birthday.

Off course to hire drivers you must like and enjoy people. It has been found that drivers will stay with a company if they are respected and appreciated. To successfully employee others I believe you must care for your team and be willing to spend the time necessary to handle whatever comes up. As a small business I can do this and so could you if you have the necessary people skills.

Some of the young drivers according to the Land Line article have trouble when older drivers realize they are only 22 years of age and own two trucks.

I've written in this book what to do after over-the-road driving. Well it can be very simple, build up a small fleet then get out of the truck and use your phone to run your business from your home or from any country you may travel to as you live the lifestyle you enjoy. I must admit I felt guilty as I swam in the warm ocean in Costa Rica while my drivers experienced black ice during a cold winter.

A bright, hard-working millennial individual or couple could with the aid of all the modern communication devices, they use at present for pleasure, build a business that could last a lifetime and then be passed on to their children.

The owners of the two largest truck stops are on the list of Forbes Billionaires. The owners of Love's Travel Stops occupy the number 205 spot at $5.9 billion and the owner of Pilot Flying J truck stops is number 771 at a net worth of $2.3 billion. So trucking has been good to both Mr. and Mrs. Love and Mr. Haslam.

This applies very much to new immigrants like we were over 20 years ago. Trucking has enabled my wife and I to live the American dream more by luck than planning. Go into trucking with a plan and when setbacks occur use them to strengthen the plan. If you are younger and healthier than we were when you start trucking and have a plan, with all the advances the internet has made possible, you will succeed.

Maybe if you get into trucking it shouldn't be until something better comes along, that something better could be trucking.

Young Couples

You've finished college after many years and you discover that work for which you are trained is hard to find. Live in the truck to avoid rent payments, and take time off at a parent's place when you feel like it.

Set a goal to get the education debt paid off and accumulate a good down payment for a home. So when the kids do arrive, you can afford to live on one income. While out driving, you can take online courses to keep your college training upgraded and refreshed. When the kids come, you can find a regular job in your field of expertise.

Maybe you never made it to college and you're not making big money, or you don't have a trade that you can always return to. Go truck driving and see the country. Live in the truck, with no costs of apartment rent or car payment, and you'll be able to save most of what you make. By the time the kids arrive you'll have saved enough money to settle into a permanent home and get out of the truck and employ drivers as you develop your trucking business.

Separating Military

In October 2008 the "Troops 2 Truckers" program was announced by the American Trucking Association. The program helps to establish a career path for active duty military personnel. To train as civilian truck drivers while still in the military, it also helps with job placement.

Werner Enterprises does not train but will hire recent graduates from truck driving schools. Werner's Web site explains how the V.A. Educational Benefit money works. This money is paid from the federal Department of Veterans Affairs directly to the driver. Once the driver is employed, it takes the V.A. about ninety days to determine eligibility and issue a check. Pay depends on a person's category, but it is all tax-free. To find out if you are eligible contact the V.A. at: (888) GI BILL1 or (888) 442-4551.

Schneider International is one of the largest employers of military personnel. Schneider pays benefits and differential pay when soldiers are deployed for up to 18 months — in other words, if the military pay is less than what the soldier was making, Schneider will pay the difference. They guarantee home time for weekend drill and annual training — no vacation time required.

Schneider International's quick-hire process allows active military to apply, interview, and be accepted up to two months prior to separation. There are nationwide opportunities for veterans throughout Schneider's network of offices, maintenance facilities, and operating centers.

Schneider International must be doing something right for veterans because 35 percent of their drivers have military backgrounds.

Con-Way Truck Load spends half a million dollars a year to support its truck drivers who are on active duty as guardsmen or reservists.

In 2014 JB Hunt made a pledge to hire 10,000 military veterans by 2020. JB Hunt recruits veterans through a program called *Hunt's Heros*.

FMCSA (Federal Motor Carrier Safety Administration) proudly supports America's Armed Services and is committed to assisting Veteran's seeking transition from US Military Service to new careers in the transportation industry.

FMCSA's efforts to support our service members are bolstered by several provisions in the Fixing America's Surface Transport Act (FAST Act) signed by President Obama in December 2015.

Military Skills Test Waiver Program makes it possible for veterans who drove heavy duty vehicles while in the US military to earn a CDL with that experience. Without having to take the road test portion of their states licensing exam.

If you or someone you know are separating from the military go to fmcsa.gov to get all the details of this new program. Their website states "Current projections show that the transportation sector needs to hire an additional 4.6 million workers in the next seven years, many of them in the trucking industry."

Single — Just You and Your Pet

Are you single and like to roam? Then get paid for doing so. Some people prefer their own company and don't appreciate having a boss looking over their shoulder. For those who like animals, most trucking firms allow pets in the cab to keep the driver company.

If you like to help people, check out the chapter on Trainers. Maybe you can make exceptional money by passing on your skills to new drivers.

For you dog lovers I know how important it is to be with your pet. Cherry and I are blessed with Knuckles, a 2 ½ year old Affenpinscher that weighs 10 pounds. While we have never had Knuckles in the truck with us we do have similar problems when we need to eat at a truck stop or any restaurant. This is how we handle not being separated. Knuckles will jump into his carry box as soon as we put it on the ground. We zip him in and carry him into the restaurant and place him on the booth seat next to one of us. Of the many times we have done this he has never even given any sign to the staff that he was present.

I took Knuckles to a friend's 65th wedding anniversary and had him at my feet for hours. I would at times carry him out in the carry bag and let him take a walk. There was a photo booth at the event for guests to take photos. I held Knuckles in my arms for the photo and when the 65th wedding couple viewed the photos it was only then they realized Knuckles was part of their celebration.

The problem with a dog in the truck is it may get destructive. We once had a Pyrenees Mountain Dog that would tear up Cherry's house plants if left without people for too long. Only yesterday a driver told me that he no longer has his do with him because it damaged the truck.

I'm quite sure this problem could be handled if a small dog was crate trained and you could have him with you in a carry bag while eating. I haven't taken Knuckles with me when I have taken a shower at a truck stop but I am quite sure it wouldn't be a problem.

As we travel with Knuckles we put down a dog training pad so if he has to go there is always a place for him to do so.

Numerous studies have shown that having a pet helps lower stress levels, decreases blood pressure, benefits our cholesterol, improves our mood and boots our immune system. In other words, lengthens our life span   What's more it's good exercise taking a dog for a walk.

Types of Jobs Available

You Can Drive a Truck Without It Bending in the Middle

So you say, "Forget it. I'll never be able to back a big rig that bends in the middle." (That mechanical bend is between the tractor and the trailer.)

If you can drive a motor home, you can drive an expediter truck. Expediter trucks can be 18-wheelers like FedEx Custom Critical but are usually straight trucks that have no trailers. Some trucks have just two axles with six wheels but the usual expediter truck has three axles with ten wheels.

An Expediter Truck

Expediter trucks have sleepers just like regular big rigs. The cargo area is about 22 feet long, making the whole truck about the size of a motor home. Expediter trucks can be equipped with an automatic shift, so it's no different than driving a motor home.

The smaller ones of a certain weight can be driven on a regular car license. The heavier ones need a Class B Commercial License, as compared to the Class A License needed to drive a big rig. With a Class C Car License, you can drive a vehicle up to a fully loaded weight of 26,000 pounds. The Class B License lets you drive a vehicle over 26,000 pounds. A Class A License is required to drive any combination of vehicles like a big rig tractor and trailer.

The expediter fleet is based around the auto industry. When a part is needed for a production line, speed is important to avoid the loss of production. Therefore, expediter trucks are driven non-stop by a team to get the production line up and running again. For good reason, expediter carriers are sometimes called the ambulance service of the trucking industry.

When the economy is booming, expediters are needed to handle the overflow that didn't fit in the space available on the regular trucks, or deliver a piece of freight that was overlooked and wasn't shipped as planned.

It is considered in the industry that expediters can spend a lot of time sitting, waiting for a load. Panther Expedited Services Inc. answers this by saying, "Just like any other area of the transport industry, there are going to be times when you're going to have downtimes between loads. Expediting is no different in this aspect from any other area of the transportation industry."

Even if an expediter sits more than other trucks, the per-mile pay is usually higher for expediting. Expediting is ideal for a husband and wife to drive together. Some firms will only have natural teams (e.g. husbands and wives). The biggest need for expediters is in the Midwest, serving the auto industry, but you will get to see the 48 states and Canada.

If you live away from the Midwest, you may spend very little time at home, but if you're with your partner this shouldn't be a problem.

If you and your wife are considering buying a motor home to see the country, look into expediting before you do so. If you are 65 or older you can become an owner-operator without having to worry about health insurance, as you have Medicare. If you're 65, you can fly with Southwest Airlines at 50 percent discount if you need to get home.

Most expediters are owner-operators, but companies are also looking for drivers to drive for their fleet owners. Some owner-operators start off with one truck and then get two or more trucks running for the same company. These are called fleet owners.

The advantage of expediting is that it's not a big rig with 18 wheels that is your home. The ten-wheeler straight truck can be driven almost anywhere. If you choose to stay in a motel, parking won't be as big a problem as parking an 18-wheeler. You can just look at it as your motor home and someone else pays for the diesel fuel as you move from one place to another. And the Class B License is a lot easier to get than a Class A License.

If this appeals to you, get a job with a fleet owner before you take the plunge to be an owner-operator. If the lifestyle appeals, you can then buy or lease your own straight truck and save the cost of running a motor home.

For more information, www.expeditersonline.com has a list of all the expediter companies.

Driving RVs You Don't Own

If you have a ¾-ton or 1-ton pickup truck, you can haul travel trailers and/or fifth-wheelers from the recreational vehicle (RV) manufacturer to the dealer. Fifth-wheel travel trailers sit on the back of a pickup just like a big-rig's trailer.

Quality Drive-Away Inc., a large transporter of RVs, says that the pick-up user must have an eight-foot bed.

You don't need a pickup to deliver motor homes to dealers. You can fly in and pick up a motor home. As you move across the country on the way to a dealership, you have a motor home to live in.

Classic Transport Ltd., another company that specializes in this field, says 50 percent of their drivers prefer to tow their own car behind the motor homes they deliver. That way, they can take their time returning home. The towed vehicle needs to weigh 3,200 pounds or less.

If you are over 65 and flying at 50 percent off on Southwest Airlines, you can see the whole country while being able to deduct the airfare as a business expense. Check this out with your tax advisor before you jump.

If this may be in your future, buy a vehicle that can be towed four wheels down behind a motor home. This is also called "dinghy towing" — just like a dinghy is towed behind a boat. For more information, go to www.motorhomemagazine.com and use the link to the Dinghy Towing Guides.

Classic Transport
www.classic-transportinc.com (866) 724-1606
Quality Drive-Away
www.qualitydriveaway.com (574) 642-2000
Horizon Transport
www.horizontransport.com (800) 320-4055

Dedicated Routes

Dedicated means set apart for special use or purpose. A dedicated route is a set route that a driver follows on a regular basis. There is much in favor of having a dedicated run. When you travel the same route, you learn where to buy food and fuel without paying too much. You have regular customers that you service, many of whom become your friends. You know exactly what your income will be, and you know exactly where you'll be in the future. When you work a regular schedule, you can plan social events because you know exactly when you'll be home.

All the things in favor of a dedicated route are also the main objections to it. If a regular customer has a thing about drivers and is hard to handle, you may be stuck with him. You'll also be driving the same route, eating at the same places, and nothing will be new anymore.

Experienced drivers who have seen and done it all sometimes settle for a dedicated route to avoid some of the hassles of sitting without work. A dedicated run can be the answer for a family man who wants to see his kids. Most dedicated runs are offered to existing drivers, but drivers new to the business can be at the right place at the right time and get hired and trained to take on a dedicated run. You may just live in a perfect location to service a dedicated run. If this appeals to you, make some inquiries to the large trucking firms.

Intermodal Truck Driving

Intermodal is where two different modes of transportation are used to get the cargo to its final destination. For example, a container can be carried by ship, then by rail or road. If a container is shipped by rail it will probably have to be transported by truck to its final destination, so intermodal truck drivers move goods to or from a port or rail yard.

The local and regional opportunities associated with intermodal allow more time at home, so it's a good choice for drivers with children who haven't left the nest.

Company Drivers

Company drivers don't own their trucks. The transport company they work for owns the trucks. They can work for the Teamsters Union and get paid a good hourly wage plus benefits. Non-union drivers get paid on a mileage basis, usually with bonuses. A 401(k) retirement plan and health care benefits can be included. Sometimes a company driver can be paid a percentage of the money the carrier receives for hauling the goods.

In-house carriers like Walmart are those companies that carry their own goods. These companies usually get their drivers home more often because they have a more predictable schedule.

Owner-Operators, Also Known as Independent Contractors

The owner-operator leases or owns his own tractor and in some cases the trailer as well. When you see a fancy sleeper, or a truck with special paint work, it will be owned by the driver. Most owner-operators are under contract to a transport company that provides them with the freight they haul. Their trucks are painted in the company colors. They are paid on a mileage basis or a percentage of what is paid for transporting the load.

The owner-operator pays for the expenses involved in running his truck. He pays for truck repairs and the diesel fuel the trucks run on. Most large companies protect their owner-operators from fuel price increases by adding a surcharge which the shipper pays when the price of diesel is high.

Some companies have both owner-operators and company-owned trucks. Other companies hire exclusively company drivers driving equipment owned by the company.

Some companies employ only owner-operators. The most notable are the van lines that move household furniture. These drivers own their tractors and, very often, own their trailers. The equipment is usually kept in first-class order, reflecting pride of ownership. This is where you see the large sleepers and the trailers that are in perfect condition.

It is very easy to become an owner-operator. Some companies will lease you a truck with no money down and no credit check. The company that I run for uses only owner-operators. They will finance a driver into a truck with a down payment of 10 percent. The loan is paid back normally over three to six years. To get sufficient drivers recently my company established a program for a new driver to lease a truck with no down payment.

Local and Regional Truck Driving

Some large carriers have regional or local fleets. If you need to get home to your family, local or regional driving will allow this to happen more frequently than driving all over the forty-eight states.

Let me Explain the Equipment

Trucks, Tractors, Big Rigs and Semis

The U.S. Department of Transport states a "truck-tractor" is a vehicle used to pull other vehicles. To make things simple, the term truck-tractor is shortened to "tractor." Tractor is the name for the part of the big rig that includes where the driver sits in the cab and where the engine is located. There is also a sleeper in the over-the-road tractor. A tractor is different from a "straight truck" where the engine, cab, and a place to carry the load is all part of a single unit. In a big rig the cargo is carried in the trailer, not the tractor.

The trailer sits over the rear wheels of the tractor, and can articulate (bend) between the truck and trailer. The tractor can be detached from the trailer. A tractor driven without pulling a trailer is called a "bobtail." Like a cat with no tail. It is a tractor that is not towing a trailer.

A tractor and trailer is also known as a "semi" which is short for semi-trailer. It's called a semi-trailer because a large portion of its weight is supported either by a tractor or by a detachable front-axle assembly known as a dolly.

A 5th Wheel Dolly

A semi-trailer is normally equipped with legs which can be lowered to support it when it is uncoupled.

In America, a tractor-trailer combination is commonly known as a big rig. A horse and carriage was known as a rig, hence a tractor and trailer is called a big rig. In England a big rig is known as an artic, short for an "articulated trailer".

I grew up on a farm and thought I knew what a tractor was: It is an agricultural pulling vehicle that pulls combines, trailers, plows, etc. I discovered that there was another type of tractor other than a farm tractor, a vehicle originally called truck-tractor that pulled a trailer down a highway.

The correct name for a big rig is "tractor and trailer," but it is commonly referred to as a truck. Truck stops are not called tractor and trailer stops. In general usage, trucks include straight truck and big rigs. A truck driver could drive either.

Why Big Rigs Are Called 18-Wheelers

Most over-the-road trucks are 18-wheelers. They usually come with a tractor that has three axles. The front axle, which is the steering axle, has two wheels. The rear, or driving, axles have four wheels on each axle (dual wheels on each side). This adds up to ten wheels on the tractor. The trailer usually has two axles with a total of eight wheels. Hence, they are called 18-wheelers.

Side view and underside view of
a **conventional 18-wheeler
semi-trailer truck**
  1. tractor unit
  2. semi-trailer (detachable)
  3. engine compartment
  4. cabin
  5. sleeper (not present in all
  trucks)
  6. air dam
  7. fuel tanks
  8. fifth wheel coupling
  9. enclosed cargo space
  10. landing gear
  11. tandem axles

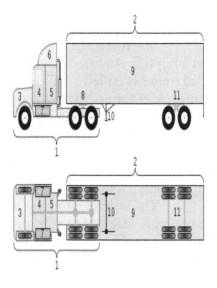

When a tractor pulls two trailers, the tractor usually has only two axles, a total of six wheels. Three axles are used on the two trailers giving a total of 12 wheels. Between the tractor and the two trailers, there are 18 wheels, the same as a one-trailer rig. Two trailers pulled at the same time are known as "doubles" in the trucking industry.

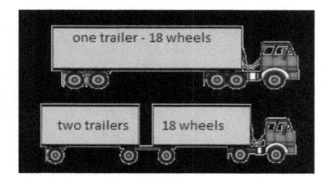

Both types of rigs, whether one or two trailers, can carry the same weight, a total of up to 80,000 pounds. This includes the weight of the tractor, trailer(s) and cargo. Some companies use two trailers because they can haul a load, drop one trailer, and then leave the other in another location. FedEx and UPS find that having the load spread over two trailers suits their purposes better than one trailer would.

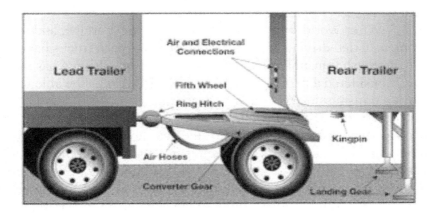

Most big rigs have one trailer because most loads get picked up at one place and are then unloaded at one final destination.

Tractor Engines

A modern tractor has a diesel engine with six cylinders. A turbo charger helps to increase power and fuel efficiency. A turbo charger is fitted to the exhaust manifold. When the burned fuel is released from the motor, its force drives a small rotor that spins at a very high speed. This spinning rotor is used to pump fresh air into the motor, and since the fresh air being drawn into the motor is under pressure the engine works more efficiently.

Transmissions Usually Have Nine or 10 Gears

Transmissions have up to 18 gears, but nine or 10 gears are the norm. The transmission does not have synchromesh, as stick shift cars do. Synchromesh is a part of the transmission that allows gears to change speed so they can mesh together without grinding when gear changes are made in a stick shift.

After World War II, Europe had a driver shortage, and many women started driving trucks. As a result, European trucks have synchromesh transmissions. In this country, truck driving has usually been considered a man's job, and a "real" driver must be able to work a transmission without synchromesh.

To change gears in a transmission without synchromesh, you need to engage the clutch and shift the gear lever to neutral — in other words, out of gear. The clutch is put in again and the gear lever is shifted to a different gear, this is "double clutching." When you double clutch while changing down, you need to "rev up" the motor about 400 revolutions per minute so the cogs in the transmission are going at the same speed. This allows the gears to engage. If this is not done quite right, a grinding of the gears will occur. If this is done really badly it will be hard to get the vehicle back in gear.

The other problem with gear changing is that the clutch is built for a man. It's hard to push in. Sometimes, smaller drivers find it difficult to work a clutch, especially while they're being trained and have to use it constantly when learning to reverse.

Truck manufacturers do provide the option to make the clutch as light as a car, but not many are sold.

Automatic Shift Transmission

Now there are automatic transmissions built for over the road tractors. Technically, tractor automatic transmissions are not like automobile automatic transmissions, where fluid is pumped to change gears. The big-rig automatic transmission is like a manual truck transmission that uses a clutch. Instead of the driver shifting gears, shifting is performed by motors controlled by a computer.

Automatic transmissions have the potential to eliminate damage due to improper shifting, thus reducing operating costs. An auto shift is programmed to shift gears at the point of greatest efficiency, improving fuel economy and reducing costs.

I believe that an auto shift has an added safety factor for a new driver. If a driver has his attention on shifting gears when he should have his attention on the road and traffic, this distraction could cause him to have accidents.

Auto shifts are being made available by a number of companies on trucks driven by teams where a lady may be one of the drivers. Some fleets that employ teams have only automatic transmission trucks. US Xpress has an automatic fleet. You may be able to get a Commercial Driver's License by driving an auto shift, then work for a company that uses auto shift transmission and never learn to drive a stick shift.

Even if you own your own truck it can have auto shift transmission. I believe that, in time, auto shifts will be widely available in most fleets due to reduced operating costs and the potential to keep a new driver safer on the road. With heavy traffic congestion in some major cities, it's much less tiring to drive an automatic in stop-start driving, whether it's your car or a large truck.

When my wife and I started driving, the modern automatic transmission was not available. However, I firmly believed that I would end up buying a truck with a Volvo European-type transmission, that had synchromesh, and no double-clutching was necessary. However, my wife quickly mastered the non-synchromesh transmission without any trouble and got to like it, so there was no reason to change.

Many driving schools will train students for a commercial license on an automatic transmission truck. This handles the problem of a driver's left leg getting tired because of a heavy clutch when learning how to reverse the truck into a loading bay.

Since my trucks can be driven by a team, I have equipped all seven tractors with automatic transmission. If a spouse wants to drive for me with their partner, the automatic transmission will be easier to learn than a manual transmission.

Three-Axle Tractors

Most over the road trucks have three axles, the front steering axle and two rear axles that drive the rear wheels. Tandem axle trucks (having two driving axles) have an inter-axle differential that enables the driver to have the power from the engine transferred equally to both axles. Without an inter-axle differential all the power would go to the wheel of least resistance. If that wheel would spin, the truck would be stuck. This happens when one wheel is caught in a rut or on a patch of ice.

When needed, an inter-axle differential splits the power evenly between the two driving axles. The driver can engage the inter-axle differential whenever there is poor traction. It's only used when needed and not engaged full time.

Air is Used to Apply the Brakes

Air is used to apply the brakes, work the windshield wipers, and for other mechanical functions in the truck. An air compressor is the best way to create the force necessary to stop an 80,000-pound big rig.

The compressor driven by the engine produces compressed air that is stored in tanks on both the tractor and the trailer. When the brakes are applied, air goes down a pipe (known as an air-line) and works the valve that releases air from the storage tanks to apply the brakes.

Once the air arrives, the brakes begin to work. It's not like a car's hydraulic brakes where the brake lines are always full of fluid, and the moment you touch the brake pedal the brakes begin to work.

The truck's air brake line is similar to a garden hose with no water in it. You turn the tap on, water runs along the hose, and after a moment, water starts coming out of the end of the hose. This is how a truck's air brakes work. You hit the brake pedal, and pressurized air goes along the air-lines, and in a moment the brakes start grabbing the wheels. A car's hydraulic brake line is like a hose full of water, so when you turn on the tap the water comes out almost instantly. The instant you touch the brake pedal; the brakes start working.

Big rigs' brakes do have air in the lines, but no pressurized air until the brake pedal is pushed. As a result, the truck doesn't begin slowing until the pressurized air arrives at each wheel's brakes. This means that if the drivers of a car and a big rig both hit their brakes at the same instant, the car's brakes work at once to slow the car, but it's longer before the truck's brakes begin to slow the truck. It takes about half a second for pressurized air to flow to the truck's brakes, after the driver hits his brake pedal. During that half-second, at 55 mph the truck will have traveled 32 more feet.

Most truck drivers realize they'll travel a greater distance after they apply the brakes, compared to a car, so they leave a bigger distance between them and the car in front of them. If car drivers understood this, they would never cut close in front of a truck.

How air brakes work is something you will need to study and understand because you will be tested on it for your CDL.

Governors Limit Truck Speed

When you look for a driving job, a good question to ask is to what speed is the truck governed.

If you have to drive at 63 mph rather than 70 mph, and are paid by the mile, you earn less per hour. For example, 70 mph at 50 cents a mile is $35.00 an hour; 63 mph at 50 cents a mile is $31.50 an hour, which is 10 percent less. So check to see what speed you'll be governed to when applying for a job. Take not only the pay per mile into account but also the speed at which the truck can travel.

Driving slower does save fuel, and when diesel fuel was expensive trucks have been governed to slower speeds. Now with the price of oil being half the price it was maybe the trucking companies will re-crunch the numbers and realize that having a truck move faster would give the driver more money and utilize them better.

Most company trucks are governed so they can't exceed a certain speed. Limiting the speed saves fuel and is also done for safety. The truck can be governed, to say, 68 miles per hour while on cruise control. By pressing the accelerator pedal, the truck speed increases three miles per hour to 71 for passing.

This is why, when you are driving the freeway, a truck will take a long time to pass another truck. The passing one is governed at only one or two mph faster than the one he is trying to pass.

Diesel Exhaust Fluid (DEF)

To meet the Environmental Protection Agency's (EPA) 2010 emission regulations, new diesel truck makers have had to reduce the amount of nitrogen oxide (NOx) that goes into the air to almost zero. The solution is Diesel Exhaust Fluid also known as DEF, a mixture of water and urea, which is a nontoxic, naturally occurring compound of nitrogen that turns into ammonia when heated.

DEF works with a Selective Catalytic Reduction (SCR) system. SCR is an after-treatment technology that treats exhaust gas downstream from the engine. Small amounts of DEF are sprayed into the exhaust stream before being passed over a catalytic converter. When DEF is mixed into the environment, dangerous nitrogen oxides, with the help of the catalytic converter, are changed into nitrogen and water vapor. Nitrogen and the water vapor are harmless components of the air we breathe.

To clean automotive emissions, we have had catalytic converters on cars for a long time. It is part of the exhaust system located under the vehicle between the engine and the muffler. The catalytic converter looks like a muffler. Selective Catalytic Reduction system is similar to a car's catalytic converter with the addition of injecting in DEF to get rid of the nasty nitrogen oxide produced by a diesel engine.

DEF is not a fuel additive. It is not mixed with the diesel fuel. New trucks have a separate DEF tank that holds about 20 gallons. Truck stops have a separate DEF pump to fill up the DEF tank on vehicles. The nozzle is smaller than the one used by the regular diesel pump to prevent a driver from mistakenly filling a DEF tank with diesel fuel. The cap of the DEF tank is clearly marked Diesel Exhaust Fuel and is colored blue to differentiate it from the diesel fuel tank.

DEF consumption (sometimes called the "dosing rate") is measured as a ratio of DEF used to the amount of diesel fuel burned. It is about 2 percent DEF to 98 percent diesel or if the truck averages 6 miles per gallon it uses about one gallon of DEF every 300 miles.

A fuel gauge on the DEF tank exists similar to a regular fuel gauge. Also, the driver gets plenty of warning via dashboard displays when he runs low on DEF. The first warning occurs when the DEF tank level drops below 10 percent filled. If the truck runs out of DEF completely, the engine power is reduced.

With DEF now being available at nearly all truck stops, and with ample warnings given when more DEF is needed, drivers usually need not worry about DEF and have little problem filling up.

SCR not only improves the quality of the air we breathe but makes truck engines more fuel efficient. Greater reliability and less maintenance are also seen. For example, running longer between oil changes saves money for truck owners. Modern trucks only need oil changes every 35,000 to 40,000 miles, a huge difference compared with the 10,000 to 12,000 miles between oil changes several years ago.

Jake Brake or Compression Brakes

Jake brake is short for Jacob's Engine Brake, also called a compression brake. This is a case when the brand name has become the common name for any engine compression brake.

The truck is slowed down by a device in the engine, which uses the engine's horsepower to decelerate the vehicle. When the engine compression brake is used, the engine will make extra noise. On downgrades in urban areas you can see signs saying "Trucks do not use engine brake," because the noise a compression brake makes is not acceptable to nearby residents.

A fully laden truck weighs 80,000 pounds. For trucks, each wheel has a brake that needs to stop over 4,000 pounds. All 18 wheels have to stop four times the weight a car's brake needs to stop. Heat is generated when brakes are applied and if too much heat is generated, the brakes will fail. When a truck needs to go down steep grades, an engine compression brake saves a lot of wear on the brakes; a compression brake should be part of your equipment if you're going to be running where there are steep grades.

Runaway Truck Ramps

Runaway trucks are a real problem in mountainous states, and because of this, runaway truck ramps are provided to stop trucks whose brakes have failed.

Most brake failures occur because the driver drove too fast and overheated his brakes trying to slow down on a steep hill. Too much heat can cause brakes to fail. I have seen inexperienced drivers going down steep grades with their trailer brakes smoking. No one ever explained to the driver to check his mirrors and slow right down if the brakes start to smoke. A driver is overusing his brakes if they are smoking, and the brakes may soon fail. At night you can actually see the brake drums glow. They can get red hot.

Runaway truck ramps are full of gravel to slow the speeding truck down, but even gravel may not always protect the truck. If the gravel is frozen solid in winter, once on the gravel the truck may end up jack-knifing. "Jack-knifing" is when the trailer tries to get ahead of the tractor, sometimes resulting in the whole rig crashing over on its side. To get out of a runaway ramp, a tow truck will be needed to haul the rig out. A runaway truck ramp is a "sand box" you don't want to play in.

Signs tell the driver how steep the grades are. The grades can be as steep as 8% which means that for every 100 feet the truck travels forward, it drops eight feet. The signs will also tell the driver how long to expect the road to keep dropping; 8 percent for the next two miles means the driver must slow right down and get into a lower gear so the engine's compression can act as a brake and help slow the truck down. The longer the decline, the slower the driver must go, because on a long decline there is more time for the brakes to get hot and fail.

Fifth Wheel

The term "fifth wheel" originates from a coupling used on horse-drawn carriages and wagons. The device allowed the front axle assembly to turn to make rounding a corner easier.

The large, round, flat surface covered in grease on the rear of the tractor is the "fifth wheel." It's a hitch that the pin of the trailer goes into to attach the trailer to the tractor. The fifth wheel sits at an angle so the trailer can slide onto it. The weight of the trailer then pushes it to a horizontal position for transport.

The fifth-wheel allows the tractor-trailer to bend in the middle. It also allows the trailer to rise or fall along with the tractor. The fifth wheel makes it possible to separate the tractor from the load carrying trailer.

The fifth-wheel must be well greased. If the fifth-wheel does not have enough grease it can make the tractor and trailer lock up. Which causes the big rig to be difficult to steer.

A recreational fifth-wheel trailer obtains its name because it is attached to the bed of a pickup truck with a fifth wheel, just like a big rig uses.

Air Suspension Gives a Good Ride

Modern tractors and most trailers have air suspension. An air compressor, powered by the engine, supplies the air for the suspension. It is kept at the proper pressure. The front axle has big leaf springs, as trucks have always had. Leaf springs are made of a number of strips of metal curved slightly upward and clamped together one above the other. The rear axle is usually a combination of a leaf spring and an air bag. An air bag is just what it says it is — a bag of air.

Sometimes on the rear axles there is no leaf spring at all, just two air bags. The air bag suspension smooths the bumps and gives a tractor a very soft ride.

In addition to air suspension, the cab of a tractor will ride on smaller air bags. This results in two systems using air to cushion the bumps in the road.

Air Seat Smooths Out the Bumps

The driver's seat, and possibly the passenger's seat, will be an air seat. For a team operation, the passenger needs to have an air seat. A lot of research has gone into seating the drivers correctly and comfortably, with maximum lumbar support.

With air springs, air ride cab, and an air seat protecting the driver from the potholes in the road, the jarring that over-the-road truck drivers used to get is a thing of the past. Of course sitting for long periods of time is not good for the back, and a driver should stop often to stretch his legs, and get the body's circulatory systems moving.

Communications

Satellite location systems are in place on most company rigs. These location systems use satellites to show the dispatchers exactly where the truck is. The system works so well that they know if you are parked at the front or back of the building. They know what hours you've run, since all activities during your day are being recorded.

The dispatcher may know the minute your trailer is unhooked. The reason that the system reports when a trailer is unhooked is to prevent hi-jacking. If a trailer is unhooked when it's not scheduled to be, the dispatcher will ask why to find out if it's being stolen.

Dispatchers know where the truck is, and the time of arrival can be estimated. With this data, a capable dispatcher can organize another load and keep the truck moving. Therefore, the driver saves time.

Satellite communication systems that track and know the locations of trucks is a great safety feature for the truck drivers and other vehicles around him. If an accident happens, the driver with a satellite system can report it and the emergency crews will be given an exact location to go to. Drivers whose trucks are carrying high security, defense type cargo can push a button and local law enforcement will be summoned to where they are.

Qualcomm developed the first satellite tractor-trailer tracking system. It included a keyboard and small computer in the truck where text messages could be sent to or from the dispatcher. Qualcomm did not include voice messaging, and the computer was fixed to the interior of the cab with screws or bolts, getting in the driver's way.

Any query from the dispatcher will appear on the driver's computer screen. The driver can respond by using his keyboard to give the answer. When the driver feels that he needs to talk on the phone to get something handled, the dispatcher is always available for him to talk to.

A newer system, SkyBitz Trailer Tracking, is connected to the trailer and does not include the tractor. As there is no device that goes in the cab of the tractor, it's not in the way of the driver.

So SkyBitz is a lot less intrusive. Even though this newer system tracks the trailer's whereabouts by satellite and records all that is going on, it seems less like Big Brother watching you, because it's part of the trailer and not the tractor.

Old-time drivers resisted the "see all, know all" intrusion of Big Brother. Some owner-operators still refuse to have a Big Brother watching because they realize the company's safety department will know every time they violate the "hours of service" regulation or exceed the speed limit. Maybe they didn't want to learn how to use one of those "newfangled computers" and were just resistant to change. After all, they liked to be able to have a dispatcher to chat with, and if that link is taken over by a computer screen they might miss having someone to talk to.

In some ways these old-time drivers may have been correct. Recently, some companies began advertising "No Qualcomm." They are using SkyBitz to track where the trailer is and cell phones to communicate with the driver.

With text messaging and the ability of smart phones to transmit a lot of information, the driver can get most of the data he needs without having to talk to a live person. What's more, even when the driver is away from the truck, a cell phone should reach him.

Electronic logs like Rand McNally have the ability to exactly position a truck to a street address. Recently a driver stopped picking up their phone and I asked my company to find the location of the tractor. When I got the address I realized he was at his daughter's home.

Rand McNally started life as a publisher of maps over 100 years ago. It has a road atlas and one specifically for trucking. It now has GPs especially for trucks as well as trip planners for all travelers. Rand McNally also made the seven electronic logging devices I have in my trucks.

Most Companies Take Pride in Their Modern Equipment

Most companies have modern equipment, sometimes no older than three years. Werner Enterprises states, "With an average truck age of 1.5 years or less, our late model equipment has added safety and technology features which allow you to efficiently and comfortably do your job."

There has been a chronic shortage of drivers for some time, and transportation companies have modernized their fleets to attract drivers. Owner-operators can, and often do, have older, well-maintained equipment.

Sleepers

The sleeper can have a large 42-inch-wide bed, 4 to 6 inch wider than a regular twin bed. Some models have two bunks, one bed above the other. There are lights to read by. Some have a small, pull-out table that can double as an "office desk." Closet space is provided for clothing. A hand basin to clean your teeth and freshen up can be part of a modern sleeper.

In recent years, engineers from truck manufacturers have spent time with drivers while actually on the road, and as a result the sleepers are very practical and well designed. International's Lonestar interior is designed like an RV. Even a hardwood floor is an option. There's a sofa bed, a pull down Murphy bed that has a 42-inch wide mattress. Seats swivel to allow a separate work area with plug-ins for laptops.

Refrigerators can be built into the sleeper, but most truckers depend on the electronic ice-less coolers. Before you buy one, check to see if you have room for it, especially if you are team driving. There are two sizes, and I have found that a smaller one doesn't get in the way, yet still has enough space to keep food and drink cool.

A 12-volt microwave oven can be installed to heat water for coffee and for cooking. Some couples carry a barbeque and stop at rest areas during summer to cook a meal.

A 12-volt electric shaver can be used in the truck, and even 12-volt electric ovens and water heaters are available. A place for a TV set is built into the sleeper. Movies can be rented in truck stops.

A power inverter can be installed in the sleeper. Inverters make 110-volt AC power from your 12-volt battery system. Inverters range from simple portable units that plug into your cigarette lighter or hard wired units permanently installed. With an inverter you can use your existing 110-volt appliance in the truck. Inverters range from 100 watts up to 4,000 watts. A toaster needs 1250 watts a microwave needs up to 1000 watt but can surge to 1500 watts when first turned on so a 1500-watt inverter will make you coffee, toast and heat up a pizza.

Air conditioning and heating is supplied to the sleeper with a set of controls in the sleeper area that can be reached while in bed.

Some rigs can even be started from the sleeper. So if the temperature drops during the night, the driver can start his engine to get more warmth into the sleeper without getting up. The heater works just like a car heater; the warmth comes from the coolant that is in the radiator and engine block. The engine must be running to get heat.

For the driver's safety, in case he is incapacitated and needs help, he has a button in the sleeper that blasts the truck's horn to attract attention. I discovered this when I was in the sleeper of a truck I was not familiar with. I was playing with the buttons. I kept blasting the horn and made it uncomfortable for my co-driver who was on duty driving.

Small diesel auxiliary engine can supply heat and cooling. Another type of Auxiliary Power Unit (APU) is all electric with additional batteries that get charged while driving and keep you cool while asleep. Diesel fired heaters that operate without the engine starting can keep the sleeper warm or cold weather.

The sleeper is always pleasantly designed and attractive to look at. Get on the Internet and check out the websites for these companies: Freightliner, International, Kenworth, Peterbuilt, Western Star and Volvo to see just how nice these new sleepers are. Better yet, go to a truck dealer and see the real thing.

Custom-Built Sleepers

With truck manufacturers now making very livable sleepers, there isn't a big market for custom sleepers as there used to be.

Most drivers get used to taking a shower at truck stops and don't want the hassle of a shower in the sleeper, mainly because of the added moisture that a shower puts into the air. A custom-built sleeper can have a shower and almost anything that a recreational vehicle has. Yes, you can even get a combination clothes washer/dryer installed, though all truck stops have washers and dryers to do your laundry, so there is no need for one in the truck. The longer the sleeper, the more difficult it is to back the rig into parking spaces at truck stops, or to get it into a tight space to load and unload.

Diesel generators that cool and heat the sleeper and keep the engine warm are usually installed in custom sleepers. With a diesel generator, it is no longer necessary to idle the engine, and you can have 120-volt electricity to run all the electrical equipment you have in your home on wheels. These generators can be installed on regular sleepers, but their initial cost is high. With the advent of laws prohibiting trucks from idling for long periods, some companies are including these auxiliary generators on their trucks.

Truck Drivers Use CB Radios

"Truckies" talk to each other on their CB radios on Channel 19. A CB is handy in extreme weather or traffic conditions. It pays to turn the CB on if conditions get bad. One driver told me he had once come into heavy fog over the Grapevine on the I-5 north of Los Angeles, and hit his brakes when someone on the CB shouted, "Stop." He avoided being involved in a huge multi-vehicle accident.

When the weather gets bad and you need to know if you should get off the road, truck drivers coming from the other direction can tell you what it's like up ahead. Even if you never go truck driving but spend a lot of time on the road, you should have a CB on hand as a safely tool.

I drove with one driver who would ask drivers coming from the other direction, "Tell me of your past, and I will tell you of your future." The CB is used to tell other drivers where law enforcement officers are.

New CBs will wirelessly link the CB to compatible cell phones, allowing the driver to use the radio's noise-canceling, hand-held microphone and 5-watt speaker to safely and comfortably conduct a phone conversation, even in a noisy truck cab.

All the Bells and Whistles

Trucks come with AM/FM CD players. A CB radio (Citizens' Band) is a must. Satellite radio means it is possible to always have something to listen to. Satellite in-motion TV can be installed, allowing the off-duty driver to watch TV as the truck is driven. An inverter will let you run you 110 volt appliances from your 12-volt battery.

A smart phone can be used to listen to music or even to download educational materials to listen to as you drive. Some of the newfangled features include satellite radios, podcasts, audio books, digital movies, DBS (direct broadcast satellite) television, Internet radio, Wi-Fi and WiMax. These are the extras you can add to a truck, whether you own it or drive a company owned truck.

When I started to drive a car, all we had was an AM radio.

Hazmat — A Quicker Way to Say Hazardous Materials

Hazmat is short for hazardous materials. When a company requires a Hazmat endorsement, they want someone who has passed a Hazmat exam and whose Commercial Driving License is endorsed to allow him to transport hazardous materials. When an official asks for the Hazmat papers, they are asking for the documents that show what hazardous material is being carried by the rig.

According to the U.S. Secretary of Transportation, a hazardous material is one that can pose an unreasonable risk to health, safety, and property when transported for business purposes. There are numerous regulations controlling the transportation of hazardous materials, with very harsh penalties for violations.

You may have been in a state where you have seen a Hazmat sign and wondered what it was all about. Trucks carrying hazardous materials are denied access to certain areas like tunnels, and signs will tell Hazmat drivers which detours to take.

Hazardous loads must have placards to explain to emergency workers which types of hazardous materials are being transported. This is in case the vehicle is involved in a collision where the driver may not be conscious enough to tell the emergency workers what the load contains.

In addition to the endorsement on his driver's license, a driver must be trained by the company he works for in the handling of the particular hazardous materials they specialize in hauling. Hazmat will need a lot more studying on your part so work on it while you learn to drive, and do the Hazmat exam when you go in to get your CDL.

Doubles, Triples and Tankers

A special exam needs to be passed to tow doubles and triples ("doubles" meaning two trailers, and "triples" meaning three trailers). It's a very easy exam which should be obtained when you get your license. The same applies for tankers (used to transport liquids) which also involves a very simple exam. So, you should get your license endorsed for doubles, triples, and tankers.

Trailers

Most van types (enclosed trailers) are 48 or 53 feet long, 8 ft. 6 in. wide and 13 ft. 6 in. high. Temperature controlled trailers known as "reefers" are the above measurements but can only be 48 feet long. When you pull one of these trailers you need to pay close attention to the heights of bridges.

"Flatbeds" are trailers without sides. They can be loaded from the side and are used to carry construction equipment, farm equipment, and things that are too large or awkward to fit into the usual van-type trailer.

Companies that drop and hook own more trailers than tractors. This allows trailers to be loaded and unloaded without a tractor involved. When a trucking company uses trains to carry trailers over long distances, they need more trailers than other companies.

As a general rule even owner-operators who own their own tractors when contracted to a transport company do not own their own trailers. This permits the owner-operator to drop one trailer and hook on to another company trailer.

Breakdown Service

Truck drivers have the backup of a breakdown service. Very large companies can have their own 24-hour breakdown service. Smaller companies contract this work to firms that specialize in handling breakdowns. Triple-A for truck drivers.

When you see a repair truck parked next to a big rig on the side of the road, there is every chance the driver has called a breakdown service.

When a driver needs help, he calls his breakdown service and tells the operator what his problem is. The service then figures out what is needed to get the truck moving. If it is a flat tire, a tire repair truck will be dispatched (with the size tire that is needed) to replace the tire. If it is a small mechanical problem, a mobile repair service will be dispatched to work on the truck.

If it is a major problem that cannot be repaired by the side of the road, a tow truck (also known as a wrecker) will be dispatched to tow the truck to the nearest facilities equipped to make the needed repairs.

A truck driver has someone available 24 hours a day to call to handle the truck when it breaks down.

Check Engine Light

What do you do if the check engine light comes on?

All modern trucks have a computer to monitor the operation of the engine. Sensors record if something is not operating correctly. As the check engine light comes on, the driver looks to see what code is showing. The code indicates the problem.

The way my drivers handle it on my 2013 Volvos if they don't understand the code, they call Volvo Action Service at 1-800-52-VOLVO. The driver provides the service center with the code number or numbers that appear when the check engine light comes on. My 2014 Volvo trucks send the code directly to the Volvo Action Service. On my Freightliner truck the Virtual Technician at Daimler.com sends me an email to tell me what codes are active in my 2015 Freightliner and how to correct it.

The Volvo service center personnel tell the driver what the code is indicating, what could be the wrong and what repairs need to be done to handle the problem. The solution may be simple as a filter needs to be changed in the near future. Or, with one of my trucks that lost power and only moved slowly, the problem turned out to be major. A tow truck was required to deliver the tractor to the nearest Volvo dealership. The engine's Electronic Control Modules (EMC), sometimes called the Engine Control Unit (ECU), had to be replaced.

As the truck was still under warranty Volvo called for the tow and paid for the towing. But I had to pay for the rental truck to deliver the goods on schedule. The dealer was too busy to service the truck until the next day.

I'm glad the ECM was replaced under warranty. The main computer that runs the engine is very expensive. My wife thinks of the ECM as the truck's brain and that is a good way to look at it. The computer keeps a record of all the times a code was triggered.

Passenger jets send any diagnostic code via satellite phone to the airline's service center. The center gathers the parts and prepares for the job. The plane can be quickly serviced on the ground. This technology is now being applied to trucks. Volvo has introduced remote diagnostics for Volvo trucks with Volvo engines to make repair work more efficient.

Here's how it works: The driver is on the road and a check engine light comes on as a diagnostic trouble code is set. Remote diagnostics send a message to Volvo Action Service via the truck's communication device. The service center then calls the driver and explains why the light is on. If repair is needed, the service center will find the closest Volvo dealer and verify the needed parts are available. This setup allows the driver to promptly return where he belongs, on the road earning money.

I believe this procedure will be a big help to drivers. Assistance for the driver will be instantly available, with the driver receiving an incoming call to tell him how to proceed. Of course, it will only speed up the repair process if Volvo dealers employ enough technicians to prevent becoming backlogged with trucks waiting for repairs.

Also, the dealership needs to carry a full line of parts. A $6 part was needed for a truck, but the dealer 100 miles away did not have the part in stock. My driver had to wait overnight in New Mexico while another of my truck drivers brought the part from California.

Types of Cargo

General Dry Goods

Probably the largest category of shipping is general cargo, carried in a 48- or 53-foot trailer 13 ft. 6 in. high by 8 ft. 6 in. wide. This covers everything from groceries to car parts. Most large companies will hire straight from truck driving school, or even have their own in-house school and train you for free, if you contract to drive for a certain length of time.

Tankers or Bulk Carriers

These 45-foot-long tankers carry liquid loads that get pumped from the tanker to a storage tank. A liquid load can surge. If the truck slows, the surge of the liquid will want to keep the truck moving. This can affect the truck handling, especially if the truck is driven too fast on a tightly curving exit ramp.

Bulk transportation means no hand unloading and no long waits at grocery warehouses. Usually, regular customers mean bulk carriers are more predictable than irregular route carriers. They are often regional, getting the driver more home time.

Car Transporters

This is another specialized field that requires experience. Like most specialized fields, the pay can be better than general dry goods. The driver needs to be able to load and chain down the cars. It can be very hard, outside work in cold weather. It takes expertise to secure the cars, and damage claims can result if cars are not secured correctly.

Enclosed auto transport for exotic show cars and the collector car community are moving fancy cars in climate controlled comfort across America. Reliable Carriers with their orange trucks and trailers seem to be the leader in this new field. Their trucks have large custom built sleepers ideal for a husband and wife to see the country in comfort while you go to interesting places for photo shoots and car shows etc. If you love cars this would make an interesting vocation but three years' experience are needed before you can get hired and realize the dream of seeing more places on the open road than you could ever plan on.

Explosives and Radioactive Materials

Hauling hazardous materials is a very good option for husband and wife teams. Explosives must have someone with the vehicle at all times who can move the rig if needed. One of you will be looking after the rig if it's loaded with explosives. While the pay is very good, you won't be eating with your partner. This doesn't mean you can't eat at the buffet. Usually you can get some food containers and fill them at the buffet and eat the food together in the truck. I've found this method handy when on a tight schedule.

To get defense clearance for this type of work you have to be a U.S. citizen. A green card will not suffice. Two years of driving experience is usually needed.

Flatbed Trailers

A flat trailer that can be loaded from the sides is called a "flat bed." They're used to haul machinery and other things that are too awkward to get into the regular van-type body. Usually experience is desired, as extra skill is needed to secure the load and to put on the tarpaulins. When you see "Tarp pay," it's extra money the driver is paid to cover the load with a tarpaulin to keep the rain off.

Flatbed drivers like the ability to get unloaded quickly. Flatbeds are usually unloaded by forklifts without having to back into a loading dock. General dry goods loaded in a van-type trailer can involve waiting for a loading dock to become available before the cargo gets unloaded.

Livestock

Transporting livestock is another specialized service where team drivers are needed to get animals moved quickly from one place to another. I've talked to ex-livestock drivers who got out when they couldn't handle young calves dying in transit.

The transportation and shipment of horses is a specialized field for truck drivers. Vans (semis) run between race tracks seasonally when the racing meets change. In Florida or California, for example, these transports run daily as runners stabled at the various tracks must be delivered to the track that is currently holding races. These are steady runs for truck drivers. Horse groomers usually ride with their animals in the trailers, so the drivers have no extra responsibilities. Cross-country transports require experience handling horses.

Reefers

Refrigerated, temperature-controlled trailers are known as "reefers." A diesel-powered refrigeration unit is fitted to the front of the trailer, which allows the temperature to be kept at the correct level for that load. Modern reefers stop and start automatically. The diesel motor of a reefer is noisy, and you have to live with it behind your sleeper. Like every noise, you can quickly learn to sleep through it.

Reefers require more responsibility because more things can go wrong. If the temperature is too high, or too low, the load can be damaged. Many truck drivers stay away from reefers because of the extra problems involved. Some drivers like the extra responsibility that is needed to always ensure their load maintains the desired temperature.

Reefers carry frozen goods and fruit and vegetables (known as produce.) When hauling produce, the driver needs to be "expert" enough not to accept an already damaged load of fruit or vegetables, because if he does he will be held responsible for the produce being damaged while in transit.

When hauling hanging meat, the load can sway and add to the motion of the vehicle.

Temperature-controlled trailers can be used to carry household goods when a wine collection or house plants cannot be exposed to extremes of temperature. A valuable art collection will always be carried in a temperature-controlled trailer. Enclosed auto transporters also have a reefer to control the temperature of the trailer.

There are advantages to having a reefer. A reefer gives you the option of hauling any type of load — from produce to furniture. You can carry loads that are not temperature controlled, as well as those that require temperature control. The name of the game in trucking is to get the miles. Less waiting for loads gives you more miles. When you get the miles, you make money.

Usually, experience is required for driving reefers but some firms will train you.

Household Goods

Household furniture is moved by van lines like United, Mayflower, Atlas, and Belkin's.

Pads, also known as blankets, are used to protect the furniture. Hence "pad-wrap" is when you're paid to cover furniture or office equipment to keep it from becoming scratched.

Most household goods drivers are owner-operators. They own their own tractor and often own their own trailer. Sometimes the drivers work for another truck driver who owns more than one truck.

Household goods owner-operators are paid on a percentage of money charged for the move. The household goods are usually packed in boxes by the agency that organized the load. The driver then employs "lumpers" to help him load his truck. The load must be packed tight to avoid movement and to get as much into the trailer as possible. A careful inventory of any existing damage to the furniture must be done. This is to ensure the owner of the furniture can't make an insurance claim for damage that was present before the furniture was moved.

Husband and wife teams work together. Many wives have never learned to drive. The actual miles traveled by the truck are low, hence there is less need for a second driver. Usually the wife can be doing the inventory while the husband supervises the loading of the truck. Wives handle the customer and the paperwork.

A lot of time is spent loading and unloading, as all the furniture must be wrapped in pads and loaded by hand. This loading and unloading by hand is good exercise and handles one of the biggest problems of truck driving — not enough physical activity to keep the weight off. As it is hard work that involves heavy lifting, only consider it if you have a strong back.

Excellent money can be made moving furniture, but things can go wrong. Drivers can end up paying for damage claims. Some loads don't pay the driver enough to make it worthwhile. If a driver can learn fast and has a good ability to figure out if the load will be profitable before accepting it, the load can pay better than most jobs.

While truck expenses may not be high, the cost of labor to help load and unload is high. Some household goods drivers only work moving furniture for nine months and take the slow winter months off. Summer is the busy season for moving household goods.

I met one young couple with college degrees who spent the winter in Colorado skiing after working hard moving furniture for nine months, making good money. If this appeals to you, check out your local moving companies. They'll tell you what their hiring policies are.

Electronics and Trade Shows

The household goods movers also have electronics and trade show fleets. The same pads used to wrap furniture are also for protecting computers, machine tools, shop fittings, medical equipment, exhibits for trade shows, and other types of furniture that require special care. Household goods is a "no growth" industry, but electronics and trade shows are still growing.

Mostly, trade shows are in the owner-operator field, and pay by the mile or on a percentage of what the load pays. Some percentage contracts allow the owner-driver to make good money; the mileage contract usually does not. It's not really geared for team drivers, as most of the shipments to trade shows are scheduled for single drivers. However, when the "exhibit house" (the place where the trade show booths are built) is behind schedule, then team drivers are needed, but this is not the rule.

Trade shows require long waits for your turn to load and unload. Usually allowances are made for this, and you are compensated for the expected wait. It does give you time to meet and get to know the other drivers. Computer shows in Las Vegas are meeting places and social events for drivers every year. Most drivers are happy to sit the show out and party.

As the loads are generally not geared to teams, it is one job a team can get if you are more interested in seeing the country than making money. It is usually owner-operators so there is no forced dispatch. I knew a couple who had the resources to pay for a truck outright. They then went into the electronics and trade show transport business and really spent some time seeing the country. As there were no truck payments, there was no pressure on having to run the miles. Other drivers will get into trade shows when their truck is paid off and only work when they want to. Summer is usually the slow period, as no trade shows are held when people are on vacation.

Trade shows are usually held in interesting cities, so if you want to see the country and not just the freeways, consider trade shows.

Getting You Behind the Wheel

What's Needed to Drive a Big Rig

To drive an over-the-road tractor and trailer you'll need a Class A Commercial Driver's License, known as a CDL. You must first have a state driver's license before you can apply for a CDL, since the CDL is an endorsement on your state license.

A medical certificate is needed to prove you are in good health. This physical will usually be required every two years. The U.S. Department of Transportation lists certain medical conditions that pose a threat to public safety. You need to consult with your medical doctor if you have questions about your health.

The company may put you through a test to see if you have the physical strength and agility to do the job. Some trucking companies will schedule a physical before you come to truck driving school or orientation. It will be scheduled at an approved clinic, and the company will pay for the physical and the cost of the drug test. (Orientation is the training a company gives to newly hired drivers to familiarize the driver with the company's procedures.) It will be scheduled at an approved clinic, and the company will pay for the physical and the cost of the drug test.

Drug and alcohol testing is mandatory for anyone enrolling in a truck driving school. This drug testing is not only for illegal drugs but also checks to see if prescription drugs are being used without a prescription from a doctor.

Before a commercial license is issued, a check is made for offenses in all the states where you have held a driver's license. Some companies check every state, some firms will not hire you if you have a felony conviction, while others won't hire you if you have had a felony conviction in the last ten years.

The Commercial Motor Vehicle Safety Act (passed in 1986 and effective since April 1, 1992) was a federal law that linked up all the states on a computer system. The intent of this act was to stop professional drivers from having more than one license.

Before this it was possible for a professional driver to lose his license because of drunken driving offenses in one state, and to get a new license in another state. The law has been effective at getting the commercial driver with alcohol problems out of the industry.

All drivers must be able to read and speak English well enough to read road signs and prepare reports and communicate with law enforcement officers and the public.

To drive all over America, you must be 21 years of age to get a Class A CDL. In most states you can start driving out of high school at 18, but to drive interstate you must be 21.

An American Trucking Association report of October 2015 on truck driver shortage states: "From a policy standpoint, lowering the interstate driving age to 18 from the current 21 would help the industry target a labor force with the country's highest unemployment rate along with diverting younger workers to the trucking industry before they find a career elsewhere." So be aware it may be possible to leave high school and drive interstate in the future but not now. A commercial pilot must be 18 years old to be paid to fly an aircraft that is carrying passengers or freight. I see no reason why an 18-year-old is not permitted to drive a truck which carries only freight not passengers if it's safe enough under federal law for a commercial pilot to do so.

You will need a current car driver's license and a social security number and be legal to work in the USA. I emigrated from New Zealand in 1994 with a green card. I could work as an over-the-road truck driver, but I could not handle explosives for the military where a security clearance is required, until I became a citizen.

Most companies' requirements are: 21 years old, a regular driver's license, and a good driving record for the last three years. Pass a drug test. Have a solid work history and have no convictions for careless or reckless driving, alcohol, or drugs. Some companies want no more than three moving violations in the last three years.

You can see from the above that your driving record for the last three years is important. If you intend to go truck driving sometime in the future, it may pay to slow down. If you have points on your license and if it is possible in your state, you need to do driver education to remove whatever points you can. Driving is a privilege that can be taken away. Too many tickets can stop you from getting a truck driving job or lose a truck driving job you have; you need to keep a relatively clean driving record. Many truck drivers disqualify themselves because of tickets and preventable accidents.

You will probably have to go out of your state to attend a truck driving school. This will then mean your license will need to be transferred to the state you train in. It's a simple procedure and the school will help you with it. You'll need a learner's license, and you must be able to answer questions about the mechanical aspects of air brakes and how the safety features of a truck work.

Before you go to school you should get a copy of your state's CDL manual from your state's license branch or DMV. You can also download a PDF version of the CDL study manual. You can also purchase CDL study courses to assist your studies. Begin studying the following: 1) general knowledge, 2) air brakes, 3) combination vehicles. You can leave Hazardous Materials for later; study that after you have your CDL permit and sit that test as you get your full CDL. A lot of jobs don't need a Hazmat, but it is good to have it if you need to switch jobs.

Once you have passed your learner's permit, you can then begin your training on how to drive a big rig. When you have your CDL, most companies will send you out to team with a trainer or mentor for some weeks.

Your Driving Skills Can Be Developed

An 18-wheeler is surprisingly easy to drive. Because you sit up high and have a good view, you can see what's happening a lot easier than sitting in a car. When turning left at an intersection, you can look over the car in front of you and see the oncoming traffic. A modern truck steers and handles very well. Drivers tell me they feel much safer driving their truck at high speed than they do driving their car.

If you don't already know, you must learn how to read the road ahead. It should be taught at truck driving school, but here are a few useful tips: You must look at least 12 seconds ahead when you are driving. The way to do this is by finding an object that you think is 12 seconds ahead, then start counting "1000 and 1, 1000 and 2" on and up to "1000 and 12." If you get to the object just as you get to "1000 and 12," you're looking the correct distance ahead. If you get there before 12 seconds, you're not looking far enough ahead. People who have never been taught to look 12 seconds ahead are usually surprised how far that is, because most drivers don't look far enough ahead.

When driving on a freeway you should be looking ahead to the brow of the next hill or where the road turns. At freeway speeds you need to look about one quarter of a mile ahead. Twelve seconds ahead, at town speeds, is about a block.

If you or your spouse is a nervous driver, it is probably because no one ever explained to you exactly where to look.

I had never taken the time to show my wife, Cherry, the correct distance to look ahead, as I had always driven when I was in the car with her. When we went team driving, I took the time to show her where to look and how to move her eyes correctly. She now tells me that she enjoys driving and would love to own a sports car so she could enjoy driving over a winding road.

I used to teach driver's education to older adults who had made many attempts to learn how to drive, but each time their instructor had failed them. I got these people confidently driving and enjoying being behind the wheel. I've written another book on this subject. It's called *How to Teach your Baby and Teen to Drive* and it shows that skills of reading the road can be learned from the passenger's seat long before a child is of legal age to get a driver's license. If you or your partner is not a confident driver, this book will help you become confident enough to drive a big rig.

I took my wife kicking and screaming (well, not quite but almost) to truck driving school, and now she's has many fond memories of meeting interesting people and places.

Trucking Magazines and Online Publications

Many trucking magazines are published and given away free at truck stops. These magazines are supported mainly by advertising from trucking firms looking for drivers. These ads will tell you what qualifications you need to get employment with different companies. The firms usually explain if they hire truck driving school graduates or if they train you themselves. They may not even hire unless you've had two years' experience.

In this modern day and age there are also online publications. You need to have TruckersNews.com (my favorite), Trucker.com, TruckingInfo.com and LandlineMag.com the official publication of the Owner-Operator Independent Drivers Association (OOIDA) delivered to your inbox. It will keep you informed of what's happening in trucking.

Not only do these magazines contain ads for drivers, many of them have interesting articles on the transport industry. You don't have to be truck driver to read these magazines. As someone who is interested in trucking, you should drop into your nearest truck stop every month and pick up the latest issues of these magazines.

For you to understand the trucking terms in these ads, I've included many words they use in the glossary in the back of this book.

Navigation

With a global positioning system (GPS) navigation system today, finding your way around is easy. Now every smart phone can be used as a navigation tool, also electronic logs like the Rand McNally model has maps that you can use to get to your destination.

When using my first navigation system we decided to give it a name after all it was talking to us and giving us directions. Hence, we are guided by Amy. Only after we named it did we realize that it was a perfect name: "Aim me."

Working out the best way to go was one of my biggest worries as I was getting trained as a driver. I resolved this quite easily without spending too much money. The Rand McNally Motor Carriers Road Atlas was recommended by many people, but I found that I used the AAA Road Atlas more often, and I only used the Rand

McNally when the AAA didn't show what I wanted.

I'd plan a route, realizing that the world is not flat, and that the full page map of the USA might not show the shortest route just by looking at it. If I was in doubt, I'd calculate the distance using the United States Driving Distance Chart in the back of the road atlas. I would calculate the distances driving through various cities. This would give me the mileage for going alternative routes.

I'd plan the route, then go to the individual maps for the states I'd be driving through to get exit numbers. From St. Louis to Atlanta I'd take the I-64 East, and at Exit 73 take the I-57 South. At Exit 44 take the I-24 South through Nashville all the way through Chattanooga, and at Exit 185 take the I-75 South to Atlanta. (I needed to carry a magnifying glass to do this.) The purpose of having the exit numbers was to make sure I didn't miss any freeways I was supposed to take. By having the exit number, you know where you must change freeways. I missed getting off a freeway once, before I started looking for the exit numbers. It put us so far behind schedule I vowed never to miss a freeway again.

Later, I bought a little electronic device that gave me the shortest route between cities. Now, of course, a smart phone or a computer will do all this, but if you are not computer literate and don't have a GPS navigation system, you can still get around it with the use of an atlas.

A regular GPS system works well on the highway, but when you get off the main road it will give you directions for a car. And may take you on roads not suitable for a big rig, hence you need a GPS system designed for large trucks.

Sometimes it pays to call ahead to get directions from someone who knows the best route for a big rig to travel on to get to your final destination.

I also keep an up-to-date copy of the National Truck Stop Directory with copies of the larger truck stop lists of locations stapled inside its cover. I'd get those lists from the major truck stop chains.

I'd use the truck stop directory to plan when to stop for fuel and food. Once again I'd write down the exit numbers so I wouldn't have to worry about missing the exits.

Backing into Loading Docks

A commercial driver's license is difficult to get because of the skill required to reverse a big rig. Even though drivers of doubles (those drivers pulling two trailers) never backup two trailers as it is impossible to do so. Some depots used yard jockeys even for single trailers to speed up moving trailers and conserve space. (Yard jockeys are a purpose built tractor designed to move trailers into loading docks in a third the time it takes an OTR tractor.) So some drivers of single trucks do not need to be able to back into a loading dock.

When a husband and wife team drives, the inexperienced driver quite often prefers to only drive the freeways. The more experienced driver will usually be the one who parks the vehicle. When reversing into tight spaces, one team member can be outside the truck with a cell phone or hand-held CB radio giving the driver directions. This is one of the reasons why teams have fewer accidents — a second person is there to guide the driver and stop him from backing into things.

If you want to go driving and your spouse doesn't want the responsibility of backing the rig, there is every possibility that he/she may never have to. The second seat driver really only needs to be able to pull in and out of a rest area or the fuel aisle at a truck stop. The first seat driver can back into loading docks and park the rig at truck stops. The tricky driving can be done by whichever partner chooses to be the first seat driver. This can be the woman or the man.

Even if you drive hard as a team, when you pull into a truck stop to eat you'll both be awake, so the first seat driver can park the rig. Most trucks can go over 1,000 miles before having to refuel, so even a hard driving team only needs to stop for fuel once a day.

Presently, government laws require the same level of commercial driving qualifications for the first seat driver and the second seat driver. But perhaps there should be a "second seat qualification" requiring a lesser degree of ability to reverse a trailer into a loading bay, as long as there is a first seat driver present in the truck. A change in the law would make it easier and more desirable for wives to drive with their husbands.

93

In New Zealand, parallel parking is not included in a driver's test. It was realized that not being able to parallel park did not cause serious accidents. Nobody died because of an inability to parallel park. I think the same thinking should apply to getting a CDL. The test should be to see if a driver is safe on the road. There is always another driver around and sometimes a yard jockey to help the driver back into a tight space. There is no help available when driving out on the road. That's where driving expertise is needed.

Job and Driving History

Any employer is going to need your job history, so you need to spend the time to get it in order.

My company asks for names, addresses, and phone numbers of present and previous employers. The month and year of when you began and ended working (e.g. Started - Sept. 2004; Left – October 2015). The position you held, the name of your supervisor, and, if not your present employment, your reason for leaving.

The employment or affiliation record is required, listing the most recent job first and stating if you are presently employed. Any gaps in employment of 30 days or more must be explained.

Once you have the job history together, you need to keep a copy of it; if you change jobs you'll have all the phone numbers and addresses available to quickly fill out a new application.

The easiest way to check your Motor Vehicle Record (MVR) is to check with the insurance company that insures your car. Your personal driving history for the last three years, including traffic violations and accidents, will be part of the application form.

My company wants to know if you have ever been convicted of a felony or a misdemeanor, or released from prison in the last ten years. They want to know if you've ever been denied the right to operate a motor vehicle, or have ever driven under the influence of alcohol or controlled substances (another term for drugs.)

To get a good driving job you will need to have a good driving record. If you intend to one day in the future go truckin', your license is very important to you. Drive smart and safe; don't get tickets, and don't wreck your future by drinking and driving.

Get Trained at No or Low Cost

Some trucking companies train at almost no cost to the new driver if you stay with the company for an agreed-upon length of time. These trucking firms all seem to promise a CDL in three weeks. You then drive with a trainer for three or more weeks to gain experience on the road.

Starting work with a company that trains you means that you will be supported by the company as you train, and then drive out with a trainer to start your new life. Also, if the company has its own school, it will need mentors or trainers to train new people. This can happen after a remarkably short time. C.R. England only requires six months' experience to become a trainer. Such large trucking firms give you this option to earn extra money as a trainer.

The companies that train in-house usually require no money down, and have no credit requirements. No cosigner is needed to get you a new profession. Upon successful completion of the training program, you are guaranteed a job as an OTR driver.

While training, you usually get paid between $350 and $500 per week, and often accommodation is provided while you get your CDL. You will need to check out these details to find a company that suits your needs.

The other factor to consider is location. Even married couples will want to get home at times. A company that offers free training and runs through or into the area where you live is what you need to look for.

I know of no other profession where you can be earning good money so quickly, with a guaranteed job after training, and have no long term education debt.

Education debt cannot be removed by bankruptcy. Americans who think they are doing the right thing are getting into debt so they can get better pay in the future then get trapped by the debt when the high paying job isn't available. This can result in spending the rest of their lives paying for their education debt. This makes truck driving look like a much better option.

Teams Learning Together

Today, once a new driver has a CDL, most trucking companies let the new driver run with a trainer for some weeks to get experience on the road.

My wife, Cherry, and I left school as a team and began our OTR adventure together. We were not split up and sent out with different trainers. We made a point of only working for a company which didn't separate us, as Cherry refused to go in a truck with a trainer.

We found it worked out well. As we were trained to get our CDLs, we discussed what we learned each day, and learned from each other. We figured it out as we went along, and as we had each other to discuss things with we managed to get it together. When we were on the road and needed help with something we hadn't come across, we asked other drivers. They saw that our uniforms were new (they still fitted us) so they realized we were fresh out of school.

We didn't have the problem of one of us being trained by one trainer and the other being trained by another, giving us two different points of view. If we had been separated in two different trucks, we would not have been in a position to discuss what we had learned or been able to reconcile the two conflicting ways of doing things.

We were responsible for each other, and there was no conflict because one was trained one way while the other was trained differently. We learned separately in school but each evening sorted out the confusions. An instructor may have taught Cherry something that I hadn't come across. Or I could fill Cherry in on something I had been trained on and she didn't quite get. If we'd gone out separately with a trainer on the road, that would not have been possible.

I believe that older couples who have worked out the problems of raising kids, etc., have the ability to sort out together the problems that arise on the road without having to run with a trainer. After all, they didn't have a trainer or mentor at home for the first six weeks of a baby's life, and the baby survived.

With more second career couples joining the industry, I think companies should look very closely at the pros and cons of separating an established husband and wife team. I think that if a couple has worked together to successfully stay married, they can learn how to run a truck without help.

Watkins Shepard is the only company I know that lets you drive straight out of school without a trainer. CRST Malone will let an experienced driver give over-the-road training to a family member or friend. Hence, no splitting up of husband and wife.

As a result of what I've written here, and as trucking managers are made aware of it, this policy may change. If you have been teaming successfully for many years as a husband and wife, and mother and father, check if they need you to run with a trainer. This is only important for a team.

A solo driver would benefit from driving with a good trainer. The driver has someone to talk with; that is, if the trainer knows how to teach. A trainer has to be selected wisely, as some do more harm than good.

Federal truck safety regulators have been working on entry-level driver training rules for years. One new proposal is for a new CDL graduate to be given 30 hours road training. Ten hours on a closed circuit course range away from other traffic. Ten hours road training and either ten hours on the road or range. With the large numbers of drivers needed to be trained this rule will undoubtedly be challenged in the courts.

If you believe that couples who have been working together for many years do not need to be separated and set up with different trainers, write to the Federal Motor Carrier Safety Administration and the Motor Carrier Safety Advisory Committee.

Trust

In trucking you must be able to trust the people you deal with. The reverse of this is just as important: you must also be trustworthy.

When you apply for a job, don't fabricate your application information. Answer the questions about felonies and DUIs honestly. For example, if you had a DUI over five years ago, the company hiring you may be okay with it. Their policy may be no DUIs in the last five years.

If you lie about something because it's not in your DMV record, the offense may be found on a criminal background check. If a court record comes up showing an offense you did not include on your application, the company will refuse to hire you on the grounds that you falsified your application.

Whatever you have on your record, be straight and up front about it when you first talk to a recruiter. Don't try to hide anything that is, or was, on public record. Most companies will let you start work, if your DMV record looks good, before they get the criminal background check back. It's very upsetting if the company then finds something you haven't disclosed and has to let you go on the grounds that you lied on your application.

The company is prepared to trust you to drive a $150,000 big rig with very little supervision. If you can't fill in some paperwork honestly, why should they risk trusting you on other things?

All your dealings with your company should be up front and honest. If this is not the way you operate, you should seek other employment where you can be closely supervised.

We go trucking to get away from a boss looking over our shoulders. We want to be our own boss and be responsible for our actions. The only way this can happen is to play the game straight.

We've seen how the mortgage industry could wreck so many lives by not being straight and honest on the paperwork and granting suspect loans. Then recently VW has sold diesel cars that don't meet environmental clean air standards resulting in massive liability for VW. No one gains by this type of practice. To get, keep, and do a good job, we must be straight and honest.

Where to Train

Getting trained by a friend who owns a big rig is not very workable because most companies will not hire you. In a lot of cases, the certificate you obtain by graduating from an approved driving school is just as important as a CDL.

If you get trained by the company you intend to work for, they may send you to an approved school. Even if you are trained by an "in house" school of a large trucking company, there is every chance that another company will not hire you because the "in house" school will not be an approved school.

If you attend an approved school, some firms will offer to reimburse your student tuition fees but usually only if they are the first company you drive for. And you are hired within 60 days of graduating from school. Therefore, it is very important that when you finish school, you immediately begin working.

Some companies will reimburse $100 a month up to $6000, so to get free training you will have to stay with them for five years. Other companies will train you in their own driving school, and if you stay on the job for the required time, training will be totally free — which is very fair, as you have gained a new profession at their expense. Other companies may require you to sign a note to repay the training cost, but only if you fail to work the length of time that you had agreed to in exchange for the training. Or, some companies may charge you for the schooling and deduct payments from your wages until it is fully paid.

If you are unemployed you may be eligible for a grant to pay for your truck driver schooling. Even if you are not on welfare you should be eligible for a student loan. Call a truck driving school near you and contact the financial aid department at the school where you intend to train.

A lot of junior colleges have CDL training programs. Check out what your state has to offer. Even Goodwill Industries of Northwest North Carolina, has a program to train truck drivers. It costs money but loans, grants and sponsorship may be available. Contact Goodwill 336-724-3621.

If you have decided on the transport company you want to

work for and they do not train you to get a CDL, let that company guide you on the school you should attend. Students who are referred to a driving school by a company may be eligible for a huge discount. Even if the firm you decide to work for does not offer student tuition reimbursement, it may offer a monetary graduation bonus that could be used to help pay off your student loan.

Truck-Driving Simulator

Many truck driver training programs have been using simulator programs for some time. They are mainly like video game consoles and pretty simple in design.

Airlines have had the benefit of very sophisticated simulators for years. As a new plane is introduced, it comes with its own simulator, so pilots can learn to fly it without leaving the ground. Just like airline pilots, truck drivers can start their training in a simulator before driving on the road. This is a huge safety factor because students will already have had time "behind the wheel" before they actually drive a real truck on the road.

A sophisticated simulator can produce driving conditions that almost never happen in real life. For example, the simulator can have the big rig being hit by cross winds of 70 mph. The simulator will train the student how to steer and brake correctly to stop the trailer from being blown on its side.

If your spouse thinks he or she will never be able to drive a big rig, he or she can now learn to do so in the safety of a simulator. Your timing on becoming a truck driver couldn't be better. High tech, in the form of a sophisticated simulator, is here to help.

Experienced Drivers

Many firms will not hire a driver unless they've had one-year OTR experience during the past three years. Don't jump into trucking unless you are in a position to actually get trained, and then be able to do at least a year full time on the road. Two years is even better, because some companies will only hire drivers with two years' experience.

The reason for this is simple. A new driver will usually cost the company money because of driving incidents, like smashing a mirror while backing into a loading dock. The more experience a driver has, the less chance of this happening, especially if he has no accidents on his record.

So experience is very valuable. It can't be bought or faked. You need to have a trucking company verify that you've worked for them.

Make sure that when you "go truckin'" your life is in order, and that you can stick with it long enough to become an experienced driver.

Here Is How the Trucking Game Is Played

Miles is the Name of the Game

The best pay package in the industry, with regards to 401(k) plan and health care benefits, can mean very little unless you can run the miles needed to bring in the money. If you intend to run as a team, only work for a company that can show you proof that their existing teams do get the miles.

Any company will be happy to hire a husband and wife to work as team drivers. Transport firms know that drivers who have their spouses with them are happier, have fewer accidents and fewer claims for damaged cargo. They also know a married couple will not want to get home as often and be willing to stay out longer.

If you are going to team drive, you don't have to accept work from the first company that wants to hire you. If a company is not set up to run teams, its booking agents will organize the loads to get them delivered in the time it takes a single driver to drive the distance. These dates may then become firm dates and may restrict you from getting there earlier when you are driving as a team.

If the carrier is in need of a team in another few days, and you happen to be the only team available in the area, then you may be kept sitting and waiting until the job is ready for you.

If it is possible, go to a truck stop and talk to the drivers who team drive. Ask them how many miles they run. Ask the company recruiter how much mileage the top teams run, and also what the average team runs. Realize that drivers will always have personal reasons for failing to run more miles. Do not expect to necessarily achieve the top drivers' mileage figures. The company may have a driver they favor just to get a high mileage performance they can brag about.

You can only make money if you do the miles, but take all things into account. If one company gives you a lot of miles, but the pay and benefits are not as good as another company's then you might be better off working for the company that averages fewer miles but gives better pay and benefits.

Whatever job you decide, don't let some recruiter give you a sales pitch. Remember, his job is to gloss over his company's weaknesses. With the advent of the Internet, it's possible to do the research to get the right job. In 1994, when we started, the only place to get the information was the recruiter, who may not have been totally truthful.

Dispatchers — Also Known as Fleet Managers

A dispatcher works with his drivers organizing loads to keep them moving. A dispatcher makes or breaks a truck driver. A good dispatcher gets you the miles. A lazy or overloaded dispatcher does not plan ahead far enough to ensure that you have another load to pick up after you unload at your destination.

A good company will employ enough dispatchers to ensure that the one who should be working for you has enough time to plan ahead and organize loads into your future. If you have to constantly wait, on hold, to speak to your dispatcher, then you know he is just coping with his job. He's only handling things at the last minute.

As a result, if there was work in the area for your company, another more efficient dispatcher would schedule the load for one of his own drivers and you'd miss out on a run. Talk to drivers from the company in which you are interested, and find out if, before they drop their present load, they know where they'll be going next.

When you spend the day trying to get your dispatcher to organize a load for you, it's harder work than driving the truck — and a lot more frustrating. For example, let's say a team has driven all night and spent most of the day trying to get a load from their dispatcher instead of sleeping. If they are then told by the dispatcher at 6 p.m. that they must drive non-stop for 14 hours to be in a scheduled destination by 8 a.m., that is downright dangerous. Yes, this happened to us 17 years ago.

Technically, we were "off duty" and should have been sleeping; instead we were on a constant "back and forth" with the dispatcher who was offering us jobs that were of no interest to team drivers. We then had to drive all night, with both drivers behind on our sleep. If the dispatcher had done his job, he would have been aware of the teams' sleep cycle and would have had another load organized much sooner.

Also, you don't need a dispatcher who ignores you all day until you unload in Houston at 2 p.m. on Friday, and then lets you sit for the weekend with nothing to do because he left work early to go on a hunting trip that Friday afternoon — without getting you your next load. You're right, this has also happened to me.

Does the company have someone on duty 24 hours a day, every day of the year? If you need help when your regular dispatcher is off duty, is there someone to call?

Most companies have drivers assigned to their own dispatchers, and you only deal with the dispatcher on duty outside regular office hours. Team drivers need more attention than single drivers because they travel twice as far, and therefore the dispatcher must organize twice the number of loads for them.

No matter how nice a person the dispatcher is, no matter how capable he is, even if he's had years of experience, if he is overworked he will not get you the miles you need to be successful. No matter how good a friend he is to you, if the company overloads him he can't service you properly. You'll get disgruntled with truck driving and want to get out of the industry because you are not making enough money.

If the company overworks its dispatchers, the situation will never improve, because the good dispatchers will simply find better jobs and leave. And new, inexperienced dispatchers will make mistakes that will cost drivers miles. Don't get a job with a company that won't spend the money to have adequate driver support. If you already work for such a company, stop being such an optimist. It will only get worse. Find a company that will organize loads, plan ahead and get you miles. Don't sit and hope — get real and get out.

Large Companies vs. Small Companies

Large companies have more loads available and in theory should be able to keep a driver moving better than a small company. If you are going to team drive, you should stay away from small companies unless they only run teams.

Sometimes a smaller, specialized company will have the work because it has regular customers who send loads out in one direction. It'll then use brokers to get you a return load. Irregular route carriers are interesting to work for when you start, because you get to see the whole country. If you get stuck too often in a location where there is no load for you to take out, consider working for a company that runs a more regular route.

The company you work for must fit all your needs. One size does not fit all. A company will run where it has depots, so check out where the company's depots or terminals are to see if this is where you want to run.

Even if you're a team, you'll probably need to get home at times, so make sure the carrier you intend to work for actually does operate where your home is.

Forced and Non-Forced Dispatch

Non-forced dispatch means you do not have to accept the load. My wife and I started out as owner-operators, transporting electronics and trade show exhibits for a household goods van line's specialized goods division.

Most owner-operators are under non-forced dispatch, but even though it sounds good, it didn't work out for us as new drivers. We started out driving in January and ended up making very little money. Looking back with hindsight, we were given all the loads other more experienced drivers had turned down. We had a sweet-talking dispatcher who would do a "sales job" on us to take a load by promising to advance the drop off date to make it viable for a team.

When I used to check at the final destination, I would find out that delivery dates were set in concrete, and the dispatcher had made no attempt to change them.

We spent those winter months running in the ice and snow of the northern states and Canada. We got lots of experience driving on ice, and we saw how beautiful Niagara Falls is when covered in ice during winter, but we made no money.

Fuel additives to stop the fuel from gelling are expensive. Windshield washer fluid to stop the ice from forming in below-zero temperatures is also costly, and we used a lot of it. We were able to tell our children that we were in Bismarck, North Dakota, the night they recorded the lowest temperature in 40 years.

We had to spend hours hammering at the trailer brakes so the wheels would turn as moisture in the drums had frozen locking them on. We learned from this that you don't set the trailer brakes when it's below freezing. Only set the tractor brakes. It was all interesting and new to us, but we didn't make any money.

Later we talked to the company's old-time drivers and found that a lot of them would refuse to have anything to do with ice and snow. When they refused these jobs, they were quickly offered other jobs in the sun where they wanted to run.

Non-forced dispatch is good for experienced drivers because it lets them run their business better. But for learners, it can give you the bad loads that the more experienced drivers have turned down.

Drop and Hook

Drop and hook, whereby you drop one trailer and hook onto another already loaded trailer, can handle the problem of reloading during weekends. The pre-loaded trailer can be left where you can get access to it in the middle of the night. Companies that specialize in drop and hook can sometimes keep you moving better than those that rely on businesses being open. When you are dealing with companies that do offer drop and hook, make sure you can get into their terminals 24 hours a day to switch trailers.

Deadhead and Bobtail

"Deadhead" is when you run with an empty trailer. This is not to be confused with "bobtail." Bobtail is when you run without a trailer. Like a bobtail cat, you have no tail. Bobtail is a good thing to avoid if you can, because without the weight of a trailer behind it, the tractor bounces all over the place.

You run deadhead when you have no load. It is "dead" running; that is, no shipper is paying for the truck to "head" out and pick up a load in another city. Deadheading is inevitable. It might only be across town to get another load, or it could be for hundreds of miles to another state to pick up your next load. Most company drivers get paid for all the miles they run, even if it is deadhead miles. Make sure that there isn't a lower rate that the recruiter forgot to tell you about for driving deadhead miles.

Transport firms don't like to run trucks empty, so they'll let you sit in hope until a load turns up. You have to insist, "Deadhead me out of here and get me some work."

You'll soon learn where the work is and to just insist. Every time I was in Florida, I ended up being deadheaded to Atlanta, Georgia, to pick up a load. Not much freight comes out of Florida unless it's produce, and that type of cargo can only be carried by a reefer.

Owner-operators are more likely to be penalized for deadhead miles. Sometimes the contract is written to pay less money for deadhead miles. Owner-operators then have the additional problem of either insisting on being deadheaded out at a very low mileage rate or sitting and waiting for a load. Of course, you can always tell the dispatcher, "Deadhead me out of here at the loaded mileage rate and get me some miles." You don't know if he has the authority to do this until you ask.

Short Miles, Practical Miles, and Hub Miles

"Short miles" (also called household goods miles) is the number of miles worked out by the computer, which gives the shortest way between two places, without necessarily following the interstate. Most companies pay on short miles and, as a result, penalize the driver. If you usually follow the interstate, you'll end up driving further than if you went the shortest distance.

If you drove from Los Angeles to Oklahoma City or Memphis on the I-40, the short miles would be fairly close to the actual miles you traveled. It's almost a straight line between these cities, and the computer would work out the same route as the one you took.

Driving from Los Angeles to St. Louis, Missouri, trucks use I-40 to Oklahoma City and then take I-44 to St. Louis. Instead, at Tucumcari in New Mexico, a computer using short miles will take you northeast on 54 through Kansas into St. Louis. It's a shorter route but it does not follow the interstate. So this is not a practical route for a truck to follow, you'd have stop at traffic lights and the drive would be slower.

You need to work out the miles you'll have to drive as you follow the interstate and not use the mileage figure the dispatcher gives you, because on a long trip it may be as much as 300 miles more. This many miles will affect your schedule and must be allowed for.

The solution to this is to be paid on "hub miles." Hub is short for "hubometer," which is a device fitted to the wheel of the tractor or trailer that measures the actual miles the vehicle travels. It's just like the odometer in a car. Very few companies pay on hub miles, and when they do they usually advertise the fact. A company paying on hub miles is probably paying 5 percent to 10 percent more than a company that does not, depending upon where you run. Sometimes a company will pay on short miles plus 5 percent, because they know they should reimburse drivers more accurately for the miles they run.

Even without taking short miles into account, you may still be penalized for miles when you drive to a city to pick up a load, and the load is 10 miles past the city. When you return with your load, this is a total of 20 miles that you are not being paid for. The solution is to be paid by zip code; companies will pay by zip code to zip code because it reflects miles the truck driver travels.

Some companies have begun to pay on "practical miles," which gives 3 percent to 5 percent more than short miles, but still less than hub miles that average 3 percent to 5 percent more than "practical route miles." Practical miles use measurements based on actual addresses or zip codes and take into account common sense alternate routing by taking the truck via the longer interstate route.

You don't have to be dependent on the miles your dispatcher gives you. You can run your own figures by using an app on your phone.

If you do get a dedicated run, make sure you're paid on the actual mileage you run. Don't let some desk-bound executive pull a number out of the computer, as there is very little chance it will be in your favor. Miles is the name of the game. If you are going to run them, make sure you get paid for every one of them.

Here's How Far a Team Can Run

Without trying to bore you, I want to give a few examples of the miles we ran each day as team drivers. I'll give you the miles we were paid for, and the miles we actually drove. I'll also give the freeway number we drove on, so you can look at a map and see how team drivers get around.

After we dropped off a load in Canada, we saw Niagara Falls covered in ice. This is how we got to the falls. On Saturday, Feb 18, we left the Las Vegas Convention Center and went cross country to Mississauga, Canada, which is near Toronto in Ontario, Canada. We only drove 83 miles on the first day of the trip — we loaded and did not leave Vegas until late in the day.

On Sunday we drove 710 miles; Monday, 746 miles; Tuesday, 693; Wednesday, 254; and Thursday, 169. The total drive was 2655 miles from Vegas to Canada, and we were paid for the short miles of

2468. The last two days were not viable because we did not drive enough miles.

The port of entry to Canada was Buffalo, New York. We had to pick up documents at the port of entry between 8 a.m. and 4 p.m. to clear customs and get unloaded in Canada, so we allowed a whole day for this. If the documents are not complete, clearing customs can be a problem. My log book shows that clearing customs took us only 1½ hours, as the documents were in order.

To get from Vegas to Canada, we drove the 93, 40, 44, 70, 71, 90 to QEW (Queen Elizabeth Way) in Canada.

I've mentioned earlier that a large computer show in Las Vegas was held annually every November. Here is how we got there one year.

Tuesday November 7th, we picked up a load from an exhibit house in Edison, New Jersey, just outside New York. Tuesday we drove 585 miles, Wednesday 1200 miles, Thursday 847 miles, which gave us a total of 2789 miles. My records show that we were paid for 2727 miles. I am not sure if we were being paid for some extra miles owed from another trip, because it seemed too good to be true that we were paid for all the miles we actually drove. We drove the 289, 78, 18, 40, and the 93 interstates.

On Thursday October 12th, we left Ontario, Calif., about 50 miles from Los Angeles, with a load of shop fittings for a new Ann Taylor shop in King of Prussia, which is very close to Philadelphia, Penn.

On Thursday we drove 287 miles, Friday 946 miles, Saturday 983 miles and Sunday 736 miles. We were paid for 2726 short miles but drove 2952 actual miles. We followed the 10 to the 20, then the 85 to the 95, and finally the 96.

On Tuesday Aug 8th, we loaded some machine tools at Temecula, Calif., between Los Angeles and San Diego on the I-15. After loading, we drove 591 miles, Wednesday 1108 miles, Thursday 849 miles, and Friday 215 miles. We arrived in Richmond, Virginia, 100 miles south of Washington DC to deliver these machine tools to AT&T by 4 am, three hours before our 7 am scheduled time of arrival for Friday Aug 11th. We drove 2763 miles, and actually got paid for 2607. We drove 156 miles more than what we got paid for, which is only about 5 percent less. We drove the 15, 79, 19, 30, 40, and 81, and the 64. We then dropped the trailer off at a truck stop and bob-tailed to visit with my wife's brother for the weekend. We parked the tractor in a regular parking space outside his condominium.

The next Monday August 14th, we picked up a broker load of tobacco from Petersburg, Virginia, about 180 miles south of Washington DC After loading we ran 260 miles, Tuesday 684 miles, Wednesday 1126 miles, and Thursday 913 miles, arriving during the night to be unloaded on Friday morning in Modesto, Calif., about 75 miles east of San Francisco. We drove a total of 2983 miles and were paid for 2858. We went north on the 95, west on the 64, 70, 25, 80, and south on the 5 to the 99.

If you've taken the time to Google this or open an atlas and have actually followed each of these trips, you'll get a good idea of how a truck driver navigates. It's simply going from one freeway to another by following the interstate numbers.

Scales

Some loads that are shipped need to be weighed. Even though the customer hires the whole space, they may still want the weight to be known. Trucks are usually weighed at truck stops. There's a book that can be purchased at truck stops that gives all the public scale locations.

When you weigh the truck empty, that's called the "lightweight." When the truck is loaded and you weigh it again, that is called a "heavyweight." The difference between the two will give the weight of the load.

Getting the truck weighed can be a hassle for household goods. You load the furniture from one home and must get a heavyweight before you load the furniture from the next home. This enables the first customer to be billed for his own weight of furniture.

A trailer is large enough to hold household goods from about three different houses. Sometimes the driver may have to drive many miles out of his way to find a set of scales.

Another reason trucks are weighed is to check that they're not overloaded or don't have too much weight on one axle.

There's a way to move the axles of the trailer to shift the load from one set of axles to another. For example, if the trailer axle is moved further back, more weight goes on the tractor. Once this has been done, the truck is re-weighed to make sure no axle carries too much weight.

Produce carriers carrying heavy fruit and vegetables have a problem with keeping each axle under the weight limit. As a specialty goods carrier, I never had a problem, since most of the loads we carried did not weigh very much. I did not have to spend time moving axles, and our lightly loaded truck would not lose much speed going uphill as heavily loaded ones do.

States have scales that trucks must enter to be weighed. States do this to make sure overloaded trucks to not damage their roads.

PrePass is a system that allows the truck to not have to pull into the weigh station. The big rig is weighed in motion as it moves down the highway and if it is not overweight a transponder in the cab flashes a green light for the truck to proceed. If a red light flashes the trucker must enter the scales.

That's why when you have been out in your car and you see a sign saying all trucks need to enter the scale some are able to keep going because they have PrePass.

Log Books

Log books traditionally are paper logs and the driver keeps his log book up to date by writing down what he has done. Electronic logging devices ELDs will be necessary after 2017. A lot of fleets already use ELDs reducing paperwork for the driver and head office.

Federal law states that it is mandatory to keep a log book. You can only drive for 11 hours without taking 10 hours off. After you've worked a combination of 14 hours, consisting of a maximum of 11 hours driving plus the time you are "on duty — not driving," you must not drive again until you've had 10 consecutive hours off. There's nothing to stop you from working longer than 11 hours, but you must not drive again. You can continue unloading a truck as long as you want to, but you can't drive again until you've had 10 consecutive hours off duty afterward. A driver must take a 30-minute break and be off duty or in the sleeper within the first 8 hours of starting his day.

OTR drivers cannot drive after working more than 70 hours in eight consecutive days without taking a day off. The 70 hours includes both driving and being "on duty — not driving." When you are loading or unloading a truck, this time is recorded in your log book as "on duty, not driving."

A driver may restart an 8 consecutive day period after taking 34 or more hours off- duty. The 34 hours must contain two periods between 1am and 5am, but this was suspended on Dec 2014.

This doesn't make sense because it doesn't fit into the normal 24-hour schedule most people function on. You can drive for 11 hours, take 10 hours off, and start driving again for another 11 hours; this is quite legal. Also, you can't take a nap, under the existing regulations without the nap being for eight hours. If you take a nap for less than eight hours, it is included in the total of fourteen hours you are on duty. Therefore, a truck driver can't stop and take a nap as he approaches a large city at rush hour. He must keep driving while tired and add to the rush hour traffic. It would be a lot less stressful if the driver could take a few hours nap and avoid the rush hour driving time, but under current regulations this is not legal.

It would make much more sense if the driver could drive for 12 hours in any 24-hour period. This is the way it is done in California, while Canada has changed it recently so a driver can drive for 13 hours. The hours of service regulations have been reviewed in hope that they can be made safer, but there are still problems.

Learn to Live with Regulations

The transportation industry has rules and regulations. The U.S. Department of Transportation (DOT) is a federal government agency that can do truck inspections. State and local law enforcement officials can inspect trucks for safety violations and log book violations.

You must have permits to run in most states, and these are usually provided by the company even if you're an owner-operator. America is not the land of the free if you drive a truck, as it's one of the most regulated activities there is.

A lot of states have weigh stations with scales that you need to drive over to check your weight. You may have to stop to show your truck registration paperwork. Some states have truck inspection stations as well, where your truck is inspected thoroughly for any safety faults. California is extremely active in this area. Mention the Banning Inspection station to any long time OTR driver and he'll have a story to tell you about it. Not only do they inspect your truck, they also go through your log book to check if it's up to date and legal. With the advent of electronic logs that the driver cannot falsify, log book inspections are less common.

If you're going to drive a truck, you'll get inspections. These inspectors don't have to first notice a violation before they inspect you: they have the right to do so regardless of the legal appearance of the rig.

In any state, you can get pulled over at a weigh station and be inspected by a local law enforcement officer. As a result of fatal accidents caused by officials inspecting trucks on the side of the road, this practice is coming to an end.

"I didn't give up my rights to get my CDL" is a sticker that one truck driver's organization is giving out — for a very good reason.

Increased Efficiency – Better Miles Per Gallon

Miles Per Gallon (mpg)

Fuel economy on my 1998 Western Star truck powered by a 550-horsepower Caterpillar engine was less than five miles per gallon. Comparatively, my 2007 Volvo with a 450-horsepower Cummins engine did less than six miles per gallon. Both of these trucks were not governed and ran with a light load across many states with 75 mph speed limits.

My 2014 Volvo with a 425-horsepower Volvo engine and the XE (Exceptional Efficiency Package) that includes $4,703 worth of extras for fuel efficiency gets seven miles per gallon.

So miles per gallon has increased 40 percent since I sold the 1998 truck in 2010. It increased 15 percent since I traded my 2007 truck in May 2012. This shows the improved fuel economy of new trucks. It is not all savings because the cost of DEF must be factored into the total expense for the new trucks.

[I know it's not quite apples versus apples. However, the trucks run the exact same route and carry the same light load. Also, the horsepower of the 1998 truck was considerably higher than what we now run.]

Even though the horsepower has gone down from 450 to 425 between the 2007 and new trucks, there is very little difference in performance.

The 2010 EPA requirement involving DEF puts less exhaust gases back into the engine. Thus, today's engines provide more torque compared with engines of the past few years.

Torque is a twisting force that tends to cause rotation so even though my new truck's engine is 25 horsepower less, there is more torque. The truck pulls up hills just as well from the driver's viewpoint as the bigger horsepower engine.

A simple way to explain the difference between torque and horsepower is that torque gets you quickly up to the speed you want, while horsepower is what keeps you at high speed. As trucks are usually governed and high speeds are not possible, the extra torque from the new engines is more important to the driver than the amount of horsepower.

Streamlining Big Rigs Does Improve MPG

I learnt about aerodynamics or how streamlined trucks move more efficiently through the air in a strange way. I needed to walk along the road to find a phone on a freeway where the trucks were moving at a fast 70-75 mpg. Some trucks generated so much wind that they almost pushed me over, but what was interesting other trucks driving at the same speed hardly affected me. What I noticed was the trucks with the square upright hoods with air filters and stacks (exhaust mufflers) on the outside of the truck were blowing me over. This type of truck was fashionable when diesel was only 99 cents per gallon. The new trucks that had been designed in a wind tunnel made hardly any wind as they passed me.

The U.S. Environmental Protection Agency (EPA) has a Verified Aerodynamic Technologies program that minimizes drag and improves air flow over the entire tractor and trailer. As a result of this program and $115 million in grants from the federal Department of Energy, it has been found that even modest changes to the air flow around a big rig increases mpg. For instance, a "truck skirt," a pair of flat panels that drop down from the trailer to redirect air away from the underbody makes it possible to have a fuel savings of up 7 percent.

Cummings mpg guide states, "Aerodynamics affect: full aero aids can improve fuel economy by 15%."

Modern Engine design has reduced the speed of the engine to save fuel. The most efficient range is only 1100 to 1200 rpm. Apparently every 100 revs per minute reduction increases fuel economy 1.5%. So reducing an engine 200 rpm gets a 3% savings. Low rolling resistant tires gets another 3% savings.

With aero aids	15%
Lower RPM	3%
Lower rolling resistant tires	3%

	21% more fuel efficient

So if a truck did 6 mpg with the modern improvements it should get 7.26mgp.

The biggest gain of course is aerodynamics and there is much research going on in this area and big rigs will become even more streamlined and fuel efficient.

With Streamlining is it Necessary to Govern Trucks?

In July 2008 diesel was $4.76/gallon, crude oil peaked at $141/barrel. But by the end of the year plunged down to $43.70 per barrel. So per mile costs at $4.76/gallon at 6 mpg was almost 80 cents per mile. As a car driver you may remember in July 2008 gas was at an all-time height of $4.11/gallon nationally. And on December 31, 2008 it was at a 5-year low of $1.61/gallon.

It was in 2008 with the surge in diesel prices that most trucking companies looked at governing their trucks to lower speeds. This did make sense because diesel was at an all-time high and expected to go higher. Even after the price of oil collapsed it still made sense to govern the trucks. The economy was in free fall and there was less freight to be moved and maybe governing the tractor not only saved money on diesel but reduced driver pay. As an extreme example if truck speed reduced from 75 mph to 60 mph driver pay is reduced 20% if the truck is running in states with a 75 mph speed limit.

This made economic sense for the carriers (not for the drivers) but things have changed since then. Fuel has always been the highest cost of running a truck. Let's look at February 2016 the average diesel price was $2.00 @ 7 mpg = 28.5 cents/mile. Now fuel is no longer the biggest cost in running a truck, driver pay is. If the driver makes $0.50 per mile plus benefits and with the possibility of driver pay having to be increased considerably fuel will quickly move from the biggest expense replaced by driver pay.

To get a driver pay increase of only 15% he would need to travel at 69 mph rather than 60 mph. Every bit of research I have done states that a truck burns 0.1mpg every mile after 55 mph hence raising from 60 to 69 mph would increase consumption from 7.5 mpg to 6.6 mpg. I think this 0.1 mpg figure does not take into account the recent advances in aerodynamics and tires, but let's use it anyway. If we go up to 69 mph it will increase fuel costs by 4 cents per mile.

Interestingly a driver paid 50 cents per mile would make $4.50 extra per hour for each hour that he drove with no extra payroll costs to the company. From what I have seen with my own new streamlined trucks I don't think the fuel consumption is significantly greater with more speed.

With the truck speed increased the driver will have less of a problem with the Hours of Service Requirements and not run out of time so easily. It will utilize the company's trucks, getting more work done from the existing fleet and not have so much pressure to hire new drivers and buy new equipment. It will make roads safer, as trucks and cars will be moving at similar speed especially those states with a 70 mph limit.

With large amounts of oil being discovered the US price of fuel must stabilize at a lower price. Drivers pay must already be a trucking company's biggest cost, not fuel.

One way to increase driver pay in the future is to let him drive more miles by letting him drive a little faster.

The very least companies could do is provide a fuel economy incentive whereby if the driver drives efficiently and gets good miles per gallon there is an increase in the speed he can drive.

Driver Shortage and Why Drivers Keep Changing Jobs

Why a Driver Shortage?

The change that made it impossible for a driver to have more than one CDL has eliminated some drivers from the industry. Tightening up on alcohol and drug testing has removed other drivers. It has been made more difficult to get a license. People who were unable to read could no longer get or keep a CDL. Driver's wages had not gone up; a solo driver could get the same pay working another job without the problems of being away from family.

A study on driver shortages, conducted by the research firm Global Insight and commissioned by the American Trucking Association, estimated that without significant recruiting and marketing adjustments, the current driver shortage could rise to 111,000 by 2014 as older workers retire. Since that report in May 2005, there's been a shift in recruiting. Drivers in the past were recruited from the ranks of those in their late twenties or early thirties after they had spent a number of years in numerous unfulfilling jobs. The result was the prospect of a lifelong driver driving for 30 to 40 years.

Now, many carriers are attracting 50-year-old-plus drivers, promoting trucking as a second or third career for mature workers who see no progress in their current profession. With the kids out of the nest, mature couples can stretch their wings and see the country (and the kids) while putting money away for retirement.

Trucking companies have improved conditions by having modern, more comfortable tractors. Carriers are making an effort to get drivers home more often and generally treat their drivers better by responding to their wishes. Recruitment efforts have expanded to include female and minority drivers. Older drivers are being actively recruited.

Modern manufacturing depends on truck drivers. The multiple handling of freight makes rail carriers impractical as an option.

A "just in time" approach has been adopted in industry where parts are no longer warehoused but arrive at the factory only when they are needed for final assembly. With trailers being used more and more as "on the road" warehouses by industry, more drivers will be needed.

U.S. natural gas prices are 80 percent lower than in Europe and 85 percent lower than in Japan. Inexpensive natural gas is giving American manufacturers a competitive advantage. Companies that have left the U.S., such as chemical and fertilizer, are returning to take advantage of the low-cost natural gas. Trucks are needed to help build these new manufacturing facilities and carry the products they produce.

With increased natural gas production because of hydraulic fracturing, gas exploration is in need of many trucks and drivers. These jobs offer regular salaries and higher wages than other driving jobs, helping to create a shortage of OTR drivers.

Medical standards to get a CDL are under review. Medical problems caused by obesity, such as sleep apnea, are being taken seriously. Drivers who have driven for 25 or 30 years, who have smoked and not cared for their health, may be disqualified and not be able to keep a CDL for health reasons.

Not only will medical requirements get stricter, drug testing will tighten up so habitual drug users cannot fake drug test results. When this happens, a lot of habitual pot smokers will be removed from the industry, thereby increasing the need for new drivers.

Until very recently pay rates have not really improved, with the exception of paying more per mile when the truck is driven by a team. At some point, driver's pay must increase substantially, this will also push up pay scales for teams as well as single drivers, as carriers will have no other option but to increase wages.

Some experts even suggest that there isn't a shortage of drivers, only a shortage of good driving jobs: the drivers we have would be able to do the job but only if they were utilized properly. There's some truth in this. While some companies complain they can't find enough drivers, these same companies have trucks with drivers sitting at truck stops, waiting to be given work.

In February 2016 Gordon Klemp of the National Transportation Institute said guaranteed pay is becoming a more common method to improve the retention rate of drivers. He said "Guaranteed pay improves turnovers and is not expensive if you do if right." Klemp noted that driver pay has seen a dramatic loss in the last 30 years relative to inflation. Annual driver pay in 1980 averaged $38,618 adjusted to today's dollars should be $110,000 a year. It should be noted that it's not just drivers who have not had a pay increase it applies to a majority of American workers.

Driver Turnover

Turnover among long haul drivers is high. Let's look at some of the reasons.

Some companies have a driver turnover rate as high as 200 percent, which means in theory that two times a year all of the drivers are replaced. In practice, it means that while many long-term drivers will stay for years, a lot of recently hired drivers will leave after a few weeks.

In many cases, it's not a shortage of drivers but retaining CDL drivers in the trucking industry. Some drivers quit trucking very quickly as they underestimate the demands involved with truck driving. It's not an easy job. It takes a capable person to handle all the obstacles truck driving can put in your way.

You may be caught in bad weather — especially in winter. Driving on icy roads is not fun, especially when you are torn between getting the load there on time or getting off the road to ensure your own safety. If possible, start your driving career in the spring so the first few months on the road aren't during a cold winter.

You must be able to go to sleep when there is an opportunity to catch a nap, or when you've reached the driving hours' limit. If you make problems of things, worrying when you should be sleeping, maybe truck driving is not for you.

You must be able to handle the confusion of a truck breaking down. The company I'm an owner-operator for requires that, if a truck can't be repaired quickly the driver has to get to a place to pick up a rental tractor and continue on. It takes a capable person to be able to handle the job when the weather is bad, accidents close the road and put you behind schedule, or you have mechanical trouble with the truck. If you get rattled easily maybe trucking is not for you.

Other drivers have to be let go because they don't act responsibly enough. They get tickets — especially speeding tickets — and have preventable accidents. Bad driving habits will disqualify a driver, and as a result of his poor decision-making ability he will have to be let go.

Some fail drug tests because they are habitual drug takers who finally get caught. Others take stimulants they are not supposed to or use someone else's prescription drugs. I've had several drivers apply to work for me who are not habitual drug users, who took a stimulant to stay awake. They wanted to deliver the load and they took drugs they should not even have considered. The chemical was picked up on a random drug test.

Of course, family situations can change and it may no longer be possible to be away from home. At times there is something at home a driver needs to handle, and the only way he can handle it is to get off the road. For this reason, I think the best prospects are empty nesters, just after their kids leave home. If that's when you start your driving career with your spouse, then by the time you are needed home to baby-sit the grandkids you will be a highly experienced team, and you can get any job you want — whereby you can be home often enough to fulfill your grandparent responsibilities.

Trucking companies employ almost three million drivers. But not all truck companies are equal. Some companies have a 200 percent turnover. The industry average driver turnover is 100 percent, according to the American Trucking Association. So it's obvious that some companies don't offer their drivers good enough working conditions to keep them.

Before you sign on with a company, check out their driver turnover rate. If they won't say what it is or if their turnover is very high, you can assume working conditions aren't good enough to keep their existing drivers, and there's no reason to expect them to suddenly improve if you join them.

The biggest loss of drivers occurs in the first 90 days. Some in the industry believe that this is because of poor orientation. Orientation is the time spent at the trucking company, learning to do the paperwork and learning the company's procedures. It includes the new driver being given a tractor to drive.

The driver is hired by a recruiter. If a bond has been formed between the new driver and the recruiter, it is lost when the driver is in orientation. Usually, just as the driver is routing out he meets his assigned fleet manager or dispatcher — often a rushed meeting because the driver is doing all he needs to get himself into a truck and leave. If the driver met his dispatcher early in his orientation and they were encouraged to get to know each other during that period, a bond could be formed to help the driver through the first 90 days when the most confusion occurs.

It's been found that drivers don't leave because of money; more often it's a lack of appreciation and respect. You need to be able to get on with your dispatcher. Early on, you must take the time to get to know each other.

A company pays over $5,000 to recruit a new driver. Don't think you're wasting your dispatcher's time if you need to sort something out. On Web sites where drivers air their complaints, one phrase often repeated is, "They lied." If you have a good relationship with your dispatcher you will not feel that he lied. He will explain why the plan has changed and, in the best interests of both the company and you the driver, what he has done to handle the problem.

If you do get into the industry, make sure you work for a company that gets their drivers the miles. It's all a matter of expectations. If the company expects every driver to do high miles, it will happen. If the company's attitude is, "What is that driver complaining about — he's already had one good job this week," get out and find someone who will run you all week.

To keep yourself happy with your new company, take the time to let your dispatcher get to know what your expectations are. If a recruiter has given you too high a level of expectations, this can be sorted out with your dispatcher so you are both on the same page and avoid unnecessary conflict in the future.

The big advantage of truck driving is that you are not micro-managed — there is no boss looking over your shoulder. If you can't get things done without someone telling you what to do every step of the way, truck driving might not be for you.

Truck driving is a very stable career if you stick with it long enough to learn the ropes. You are responsible for the decisions you make, and as long as you have a reasonable amount of common sense, you won't get into trouble with speeding convictions and logbook violations. With the advent of electronic log books, it makes logbook violations almost a thing of the past.

After about two years on the job, with a clean record, you will have the ability to always get a job in a stable industry. The American economy is dependent on trucks. It's one job that cannot be outsourced overseas.

Text Messages and Driver Turnover

Was replacing the telephone with a keyboard the reason that drivers no longer have loyalty to their companies? Let's first look at how it was done before satellites made it possible to have a keyboard in the truck.

In the event of something going badly wrong, there was no record of what was actually said with telephoned instructions. Did the dispatcher actually dispatch the truck to the wrong state, e.g. Springfield, Missouri, instead of Springfield, Michigan, or did the driver misunderstand and get it wrong? Truck stops used to sell Dispatcher Buster tape recorders so you could tape what the instructions were. If the dispatcher misdirected you, you would have evidence.

With a record being kept of the text message instruction, when the driver goofs and doesn't follow the instructions, it is made very apparent to the driver that it is his mistake.

Hence, not only does the text message make it a very impersonal relationship between the driver and his dispatcher, text messages don't have the friendly voice of a dispatcher sorting out what's wrong. As a driver, I know I resisted an incoming impersonal text message, and I would respond by phone rather than text.

When a driver feels that he needs to be debriefed and wants to get something handled, the dispatcher should always be available for him to talk to. I'm sure that this doesn't happen with a lot of drivers. They just let their resentment build, then change companies, going from one job to another.

It costs more in wages for a company to have drivers talk to their dispatchers — personal touches are always expensive to provide — but Qualcomm is also an expensive system. Maybe if, as I believe, retention of drivers is better with the personal touch of a telephone, more companies will stop relying on the keyboard and get back to the phone. This will apply especially to those people who haven't grown up using text messages and e-mail. It also applies to folks that read with difficulty or have poor comprehension of written material. They read, but not easily or happily.

As a new driver, you will need help to sort through the ins and outs of the way your company operates. If you are happy to do this by text messaging, that's great. Do so.

If you are more comfortable on the phone, realize that and find a company where you can talk to your dispatcher. Or a company that can assign you a mentor as you gain experience.

I have found it best to have a dispatcher assigned to individual drivers. It's only when your dispatcher is at lunch, or busy, that you get involved with another person. This allows you to build rapport, and your dispatcher knows how you want to run and will get you loads accordingly. He will know where you live, and whenever he sees a load going near your home he will get it for you. He knows how long you've been out, and when you expect to be home next.

I believe that if you have a good relationship with your dispatcher, you will stay with the company. People don't leave companies, they leave managers. So if the two of you can't get on, you will go looking for another job. It's usually not what is making you unhappy, it's who. The research done by Strategic Programs Inc., who interviewed drivers who had left jobs, found that drivers would return to their old companies under different managers. It's a lot easier to change dispatchers than to change jobs. Voice your concern to management if you can't work with a dispatcher, before you race off to get another job.

But before this happens, get on the phone and try to talk it out with your dispatcher. Better yet, get a load that takes you past headquarters. Stop and talk to those whom you work with. I've found that they are there to help, and I've always managed to sort out my problems. I've been with the same company since 1994, now my daughter Shelley is helping me manage our drivers.

Perhaps companies should be paying bonuses to dispatchers who manage their drivers without a high turnover. The turnover needs to be in managers who don't have enough skill or charm to keep their drivers happy.

Some companies employ a mentor for the driver to talk to someone. Mentors help new drivers who are frustrated and need solutions. Schneider International currently has a mentoring program for teams. These mentors are either current drivers or previous, top-performing company teams.

Do Your Best to Get It Right the First Time

Most people don't like change and will stay with a job even though they know they would do better elsewhere. We all seem to be optimists at heart and always hope that things will get better.

My wife and I made this mistake when we first got into trucking. We didn't wish to be placed with a trainer and separated for a number of weeks; therefore, we didn't start with the company we had originally chosen to drive for. We also didn't want to get into debt with student loans, so we started with the company who trained us for free, and had no over-the-road training requirements that would separate us once we got our CDL. Of course, we stayed with the company we started with and continued with them in the hope that things would get better. They really weren't equipped to give a team enough miles, because most of their loads were scheduled for single drivers.

Having to return a truck to headquarters and then move all our gear to pick up a truck somewhere else was too difficult to confront. It was easier to just do one more time out and hope that things would get better. Of course they never did. There would be an effort to keep us moving and we'd have a good week, so that would hook us into staying on.

We would have been wiser to obtain a student loan, and pay for our truck driving school. We'd have ended up working for a company who ran mainly with teams and we would have been given the miles. We would have made a lot more money in the long run, even after paying off our student loans.

Now with the help of this book and being able to research for jobs on the Internet, a better decision can be made than we made in 1994 when we first got into the business. Mature potential drivers usually do extensive research before they make a move, so you should be in a better position to make the right move, especially since you're reading this book.

Like most people, we took the easy way out. After all, we had friends in the company, and the company looked after us and respected our wishes. But we were not making money. Trucking firms know that people resist change. They know they can sweet talk a driver to stay on, even when they're too stupid or mean to provide decent support staff to enable their drivers to get the miles and make some money.

Not working for a company that specialized in teams turned out all right in the end. We were offered a dedicated team run from St. Louis to Los Angeles. Also, not being run by a division that handled only teams gave me an invaluable experience that I could write about in this book. So if you are a team, you won't make the mistake we made and will work for a company that handles its teams separately.

Staying Awake and Alive

Staying Awake

Apart from the usual coffee, there are other methods to keep awake.

Japanese researchers found the best method to stay awake is to chew gum. They even said the sugarless gum did a little better job than the sugar type. I chew a lot of gum when I'm on the road. One, to keep alert, and also to suppress my appetite so I don't have to eat too often. When I feel hungry, I chew gum and it seems to satisfy me for a while.

Having something to squeeze with the hand and then release gives a little bit of exercise if you start nodding off. A stress ball is good.

One driver I've driven with has drumsticks and beats time to the music he's listening to. Music is also supposed to keep you awake. Another driver hated country music so he started listening to it to stay awake. I don't know if it helped him stay awake but he sure became a country fan.

Modern research has found that classical music will raise a person's IQ if listened to just before an IQ test. I took this to mean that if it makes people more capable of answering an IQ test it keeps them awake. My wife likes to play Mozart and it does make her stay more alert. I resisted that for a long time, but now, to stay awake, I listen to classical music.

Take a nap when you can. A ninety-minute daytime nap helps speed up the process of memory consolidation, according to recent studies at the University of Haifa, Israel. Long term memory stays with you. Therefore, when you need to wait, take a nap.

I tell the guys in the warehouse to run a forklift into my trailer to wake me up when the shipment I'm waiting for arrives. You have a sleeper as part of your truck — use it every chance you get to take a nap. Not many professions provide a bed at work. Use it to stay safe.

The body has recurring daily cycles that affect body temperature. Recent research has shown that these temperature cycles affect sleep. The best time to drive is when the body temperature is high, because that's when we're most alert. When the body temperature is lowered, we feel more inclined to sleep.

The body's temperature starts to rise at 5 a.m. and continues to rise until mid-afternoon, when it drops down until 6 to 6:30 pm. Then it will rise again until 10 to 10:30 p.m. and then start dropping again, reaching its lowest level at 2 to 2:30 a.m.

This helps to explain the mid-afternoon grogginess that some people attribute to eating too big a lunch. It means that mid-afternoon is a good time to take a nap, like people living near the equator have always done. Their "siesta" is built into the workday schedule in hot climates.

There's another thing you should know about body temperature cycles. Their compelling urges for you to sleep are at their maximum to keep you asleep during the hour just before you normally wake up. Hence, if you're driving late at night, you can find yourself fighting sleep (trying to stay awake) in the "wee" hours of the morning (1 a.m. to 4 a.m.), even more so during the hour before you usually get up.

Another point to note about these natural sleep cycles is this: The hour before you normally go to bed is the time of day you may feel the least need for sleep. The body's cycles are working to keep you awake. That's why going to bed an hour earlier on a Sunday night doesn't always result in going straight to sleep. That's been given a name: "Sunday Insomnia."

Drivers need to know that an hour before their usual bedtime is not a good time to start a trip. Even if you feel very alert and bright, it won't last. You'll start feeling sleepy within an hour or two.

Take a Nap

To be an alert driver you must understand napping. A study by NASA on sleepy military pilots and astronauts found that a (40 minute) nap improved performance by 34% and alertness 100%. The National Sleep Foundation states "a short nap of 20-30 minutes can help to improve mood, alertness and performance."

A short nap of 20 to 30 minutes has been called a power nap. Power naps of less than 30 minutes, even 6 to 10 minutes restore wakefulness and increase performance. In naps of longer than 30 minutes you may enter deeper stages of sleep that results in drowsiness upon waking but once the period of impaired alertness is shaken off you will get the full benefit of the nap.

A stimulant or caffeine nap was discovered by British researchers to be the more effective for improving post nap alertness compared to just coffee or a nap. It sounds strange but if you drink coffee before you take your nap caffeine in coffee takes up to ½ an hour to have the alerting effect so if a short nap is taken just after drinking coffee it won't interfere with your ability to go to sleep. One report was that the coffee and the nap provided a double shot of energy. The research was done on mildly sleep deprived drivers even if they had trouble falling asleep, who were tested in a driving simulator.

This is important data that drivers should know and apply. OTR drivers have a bed within inches of their workspace. It's the only profession I know that supplies a bed that's ideal to take a nap. It's also one of the professions that if you nod off at work it can be fatal. So do your own research on napping so you can fully understand how naps can keep you safe on the road.

Eye Movements to Stay Awake

As a driving instructor I would train my students to look at and focus their eyes on a nearby object — then have them look ahead and find another object to focus on. I did this to get the student to take in the whole scene. I found that if they did not focus their eyes and only briefly scanned, they could miss seeing things. That's why, at an accident, someone often says, "I looked and didn't see you." (This data is fully explained in my book, *How to Teach Your Baby and Teen to Drive*.)

Whenever I became tired while driving and found myself fixating on the road ahead, I would use the above technique of looking at an object in the distance, focusing my eyes on it, then looking at and focusing on something close by. I found this made me more alert and woke me up.

Science now agrees with me, having found through tests that measure electrical activity in the brain, that eye movements affect brain function.

It seems that the optic nerves directly link the eyes and brain. Therefore, you can instantly improve your alertness with a few simple eye motions and that's basically doing what I do to keep myself alert as I drive.

If too much use of the computer is causing brain fog, look up and focus your eyes on something twenty feet away, then focus on something closer. Then away again until the fog clears.

If looking into the distance while you drive is sending you to sleep, then look and focus your eyes on something close by. Then find another object to focus on at a different distance. Continue doing this until you are more alert. Of course, if you are really tired, you must look for a place to stop so you can sleep or change drivers. It also works when your body is insisting that you stay asleep because it's an hour before your usual wake up time. These eye movements will shake off the fogginess and let you drive for the rest of the day.

To fall asleep faster, shut your eyes and roll them upward as far as they can go, as if you are looking at a point in your forehead. Research shows that when your eyes are rolled upward, it helps you unwind.

Multitasking Can Keep You Awake

The following is an excerpt from my book *How to Teach Your Baby and Teen to Drive.*

New research from England shows that some people while listening when doodling (drawing random things on a piece of paper) can recall what they were listening to better than those who were not doodling.

The research found that someone doing a boring task may have their mind wander and start to daydream. Daydreaming may distract them from the task at hand. As a result, they will not handle a task as well or drive as safely as they should.

This explained a lot to me. While driving in light traffic, I can listen to instructional type lectures and have no trouble understanding and remembering the new concepts that I am taught. I can keep my attention on what the speaker is saying without daydreaming. When I have the mindless task of driving the open freeway, it's a lot like the doodling example. I drive and listen, just like listening on the phone while doodling increases one's concentration.

I have also found that I cannot listen to instructional lectures at home when all I do is sit and listen. My mind starts to wander and I daydream.

How does all this apply to driving? I have had drivers who can only concentrate on driving, without even a radio playing. I am like this. When traffic is heavy, I turn the radio off and do nothing that may interfere with my concentration on driving.

I once turned the radio off when I thought an inexperienced female truck driver needed to concentrate on traffic and find the exit we were looking for. This action of mine upset her. I thought that she was a very irresponsible driver that was trying to do too many things at once. This recent research suggests that she was not being irresponsible because she could concentrate better with background music.

Music and singing throughout history have been a part of mindless work. Slaves sang while picking cotton and almost all cultures have had singing as part of their work. Even soldiers have sung while marching.

I did further research and found that women seem to have a better ability to multitask than men. This makes sense if we look back to living in caves when we were hunters and gatherers. The men were the hunters who needed, without any other distractions, to concentrate on the kill. The women did the gathering of seeds and edible plants as well as cooking while always having their attention split between their work and what the children were doing. After all, she couldn't let a child fall into the fire or be eaten by a wild animal as she did her work.

As time evolved, women would knit or create handcrafts or even iron as they talked or helped with the children's homework. With the advent of the Internet and e-mail, those who like to multitask will check their in-box or play solitaire on the computer as they chat on the phone.

Older brothers and fathers who have spent time looking after young children will be more inclined to multitask, as they have learned to do things while keeping an eye on the kids. My son tells me that if he wants to have a serious conversation with his sister he has found that it is best to talk to her as she works in the kitchen. He has found he can hold her attention better if she is doing something with her hands while she listens.

I have learned not to cause an upset by turning the TV off so my granddaughter can concentrate solely on her homework. It seems she does her homework better when she is watching a mindless TV show.

For a long time, I considered that being in a car together increases conversation. Now it seems that it is not just being in a small space together. Rather, it is also viewing changing scenery, even while a passenger, that creates the mindless doodling-type distraction that increases concentration for the important conversation that can take place in a car.

How does this apply to driving safety? I now realize we operate in two different modes, and I think of them as the "hunter mode" and the "gatherer mode."

When I am driving and need to concentrate, I am in the hunter mode. I need to turn the radio off or stop taking on the phone or to a passenger. In the same way as a hunter goes for a kill, I concentrate my attention on exactly what I am doing so I don't get killed.

When there is little traffic and the road is long and straight, driving can become a mindless job. When I find my attention wandering, I realize that I need to operate in a gatherer mode so I split my attention between the road and some other task. This is when I will try to find something of interest on the radio or control daydreaming by deliberately thinking through some idea while I drive.

One of my drivers will chat to his wife on the phone to stop daydreaming and nodding off and going to sleep, when not much is happening on the road to keep his attention fixed.

I should have let my kids doodle when I was trying to explain things. They would have better recalled my words of wisdom, and I may even have produced an artist to illustrate my writings.

To make safe drivers, explain to your kids when you should drive in the hunter mode and when you should operate in the gatherer mode. Your kids will then not interrupt you when they see you need to keep your attention on traffic but will understand why you can play games and chat when traffic is light.

The Most Dangerous Place to Drive is Near Home

It's surprising how many accidents happen when the driver is on familiar roads that are close to home. An OTR driver returning home is in a hurry to get there to be with his family. He has his thoughts on home and what awaits him there, and may not have enough attention on the road. He knows the road like the back of his hand, so he doesn't feel the need to pay as much attention as he should. If roadwork or some change has occurred since he last traveled it, he'll not have his attention on the road enough to notice the changes. With these three elements against him, he has to be extra careful.

So, when you're near home, don't speed to get there. Sure, think of your loved ones, but keep your attention on the road. Realize that you are probably pushing hard to get home and you may be tired, so watch the road signs. Something may have changed since you were home last.

Life on the Road

Compatibility with Your Partner

I've met a lady who thought she had a good relationship with her husband, until team driving destroyed the marriage. Before driving they had spent very little time together, and only by being together all the time did she realize how difficult he was to live with.

This is not the usual. Team driving usually evolves into a pretty honest relationship, where you care for each other, be it your spouse or another person. After all, you put your life in another's hands when you sleep. You therefore care for that person. You make sure they're rested before they drive. You don't fight with them. As there is no other person present, like a mother-in-law who may cause conflict in the marriage, there is no third person stirring up trouble.

As team drivers we have a job to do that can, at times, be life threatening. To stay alive, we must totally support and care for each other. No matter how tired we are, the most important thing is to look after each other's wellbeing.

My rule is very firm. You can fight with your spouse at home. But never, ever fight with your teammate while in the truck together. It's your job to support one another to keep everyone safe on the road.

It's just the two of you — with a purpose — to get the job done.

You may want to team drive but have no other half, or your spouse has other duties and is not currently in a position to play a significant role as a team driver. Many trucking firms that specialize in teams will provide someone for you to run with.

24 Hours a Day

Trucking services operate 24 hours a day. Truck stops never close, and if they have a service bay it's usually open around the clock. A lot of truck dealers' service departments are open extended hours, and many of them are open 24 hours a day. Most large dealerships have a shower available for a driver to use while his truck is being worked on (though you may have to supply your own towel). Some even have a bunk where you can catch a nap.

Large transport companies operate their depots 24 hours a day. If you carry freight to airports, you can usually have 24-hour access.

Truck drivers soon learn to catch a nap when things slow down. As a specialized carrier I would, at times, be scheduled to load out of a trade show at midnight. The show would end at 6 p.m.; six hours later the booths would be dismantled and the trucks could start loading. I've helped place pads around items that couldn't be crated, and finished loading to start driving at dawn. This job is definitely not 9 to 5.

Christians are Not Alone on the Road

With the advent of modern technology, it is now possible to listen to audio versions of the bible as you drive or listen to your favorite preacher to help you build on your Christian experience.

Christian truckers have their own CB channel. You can even drive for a company that shares your beliefs. Many truck stops have chapels (usually converted trailers) parked very close to everything. Christian newsletters get distributed through truck stops.

Chaplains do a good job of giving counsel to the lonely and dispirited. Truck driving can be tough on a solo driver who is always away from his family, so chaplains serve at truck stops. I've seen drivers who were upset about family problems being counseled in truck stops by clergy who cared. And it's not only Christians who receive their help, as it is also available to those of little or no faith, or of other faiths.

Many people have been called to minister to truckers' spiritual needs. I'm sure that most truck drivers will never need to unburden their problems to a stranger. On the other hand, it's always comforting to know that if the worst happens, there may be someone at a truck stop who will care enough to take time to help.

Do you need to answer the call of God and train as a minister? Drive for a company built on strong Christian values, and earn enough money to support yourself while training. If your calling is to do missionary service, I'm quite sure your company will give you a leave of absence if and when you go overseas to help those who are not as fortunate as yourself. And maybe your missionary work won't be in deepest Africa. Maybe it will be at your local truck stop.

Rest Areas

Rest areas have vending machines, rest rooms, and telephones. Sometimes a small trailer provided by a local group will give drivers a free cup of coffee. In a Florida rest area, there was a trailer with no one in attendance, and the janitor saw me looking at it, so he offered me a cup of his own coffee. This could only happen in Florida where they are very conscious of travelers' safety and provide armed night team security, if they have no 24-hour security.

Usually, there are two separate rest rooms in large rest areas. This enables one to be closed while being cleaned. In California, I looked up and saw that one restroom was for women, and then was stopped from walking into the other restroom — also for women.

On turnpikes where you pay a toll, the rest areas will have places that sell food and fuel. You won't find a $1.00 menu, like at fast food outlets; the food prices are extremely high. Tell them you are a truck driver and ask for a discount card.

In the East, it is very difficult to find a space in a rest area at night. No spaces are reserved for 30-minute parking, and if you are team driving and you need to use the rest room there is often no room to park. If you need to get some sleep, you can't depend on finding a place to park. Truck drivers need to pull over and park when they're tired, and lack of spaces in rest areas is a safety hazard.

Usually, when a rest area doesn't have restroom facilities,

they're called picnic areas or parking areas. Rest areas are easier to park in, provided there is room. You usually just drive into a parking space and pull straight out when you leave.

In most truck stops you have to back into a very tight space. I used to drive all night, so my wife would be the one to figure out where she was in the morning if I had parked the truck and gone to sleep. I found that when I stopped for the night, rest areas were a lot easier for her to drive out of in the morning.

More Than One Truck

There are many opportunities in trucking, and OTR driving will be a base you can build on. OTR driving could be a springboard into owning more than one truck.

Some people start driving, become owner-operators, then buy another truck, and hire another driver to run the second truck. I now run seven trucks employing drivers to keep them moving.

We'd often meet a driver who worked for an owner-operator with more than one truck, or we'd meet someone who owned four or five trucks and employed other drivers. It's a very common investment. I've employed a driver who worked for someone who operated six trucks. The operator of the trucks did not have a CDL and had never driven one of his tractors. There's a lot of entrepreneurship in the industry, and room to advance and grow economically.

In trucking magazines, companies advertise for owner-operators or for fleets of up to ten trucks. When advertising for owner-operators, quite often they state that they are hiring drivers for fleet owners. Many drivers start off as owner- operators and build up a fleet of trucks. These fleets are then hired out to a large trucking firm who provides the work.

Household goods drivers can learn the ins and outs of furniture removal and end up establishing their own agency. An agency can simply be an office where telephones are answered in response to advertising, and quotes are given for furniture removal.

But usually an agency has its own warehouse and straight trucks that are used for local moves. I've met drivers on the road who intend to have their own agency within a few short years. From what I've observed, these agencies seem to be doing very well. The aggressive owners keep moving into larger buildings and have very nice facilities.

Other drivers have even started their own transportation companies. J.B. Hunt started out in the trucking industry almost by accident, and is now an over three billion dollars a year company with 12,000 tractors and 16,000 employees.

In 1970, Prime Inc. had one truck. At age 20, Robert Low was the business owner of Prime. By the time he was 30, Prime was grossing $50 million a year. Prime, Inc. is the 28th largest trucking company in the US based on revenue.

Just a driving job? I'd say that J.B. Hunt and Robert Low would say no.

Owner-Operator — First Understand the Business

Owner-operators buy or lease their own tractors and contract to a transport company to provide the work. There are many programs that will let you lease a tractor with no money down and no credit check. Whether these owner-operator drivers are making money is not easy to tell. Is the owner-operator program a way to get rid of used company tractors at a good price to new recruits? Who knows?

Some companies use bait and switch: they hire a driver as a company driver, then tell the driver there are no company jobs available, but, if they want to lease-purchase a truck, they will be able to go to work right away. Obamacare has made it mandatory for employers with 50 or more full time employees to provide health care. A lease-purchase gets around this law by saying the driver is self-employed.

I have employed a number of drivers (some who have had years of experience) who got involved with a lease purchases and had very unsatisfactory experiences. Also with a lease purchase they got in trouble with the IRS because they didn't do the necessary tax returns.

I've seen drivers become owner-operators spending their money on dirt bikes and other toys and not putting money aside for taxes or truck maintenance. They end up having to get out of the business altogether because of huge tax liabilities or because they can't afford to do needed repair work on the truck.

A good rule is to stay away from a lease-purchase until you really understand the business of trucking. Join OOIDA and do their management courses and understand the tax liabilities of being self-employed.

As an owner-operator you might end up with little or no money at the end of the week. All the money you earn could be used to make payments on the tractor lease or purchase, insurance, permits, and base plate. The base plate is the tractor registration that pays for the license tag.

Sometimes an owner-operator may not even get a paycheck, and he may end up deeper in debt because of some unplanned repairs. There is also the possibility that the driver did not get enough miles to make his truck payments, yet the contract was written that the driver could not take his truck to a different company.

This is the way I started, and I wouldn't recommend it. If I were to start again, I would become a company driver. A company driver gets health benefits, and half his social security payments are paid. He gets money every week (even if he sits, he should get a little layover pay) and he doesn't run the risks of high repair costs if something breaks. As an owner-operator, non-forced dispatch sounds good, but it can leave you, an inexperienced driver, ending up with the loads that experienced drivers have turned down.

Don't become an owner-operator just because you like to do your own thing. As a company driver, you'll probably do your own thing anyway. As long as you produce and put in the miles, you'll get to live your own way.

Don't become an owner-operator if you have no understanding of machinery. Successful owner-operators know enough about vehicles to service them or get them serviced correctly. Some very successful owner-operators run well-maintained older vehicles that are a joy to behold.

There are some good owner-operator driver contracts out there. Get some OTR experience, talk to other drivers, and save some money before you jump into buying a tractor.

Most important, save money and work on repairing your credit. The good owner-operator contract probably won't have carrier financing for trucks, and you'll have to deal with an outside lender. If you have some money saved and do find a good contract as an owner-operator, you'll be in a good position to pay 20 percent down on a new tractor with a warranty.

The days are over when owner-operators had conventional trucks and all the company drivers rode in cab-overs. Now a company driver probably drives a more modern, better equipped truck than a lot of owner-operators.

Only when you understand the industry should you move away from being a company driver. This of course takes time and study, not just sitting behind the wheel. If you or your family depend on health insurance, then you should stay on as a company driver just to maintain health insurance.

If you're ex-military and have free medical with the VA, have Medicare, or if your wife gets free medical with her job and healthcare isn't important, you can look into owner-operator sooner.

Once you have learned the ins and outs of how to be a company driver, you can consider becoming an owner-operator with a company that pays a percentage of the revenue. The advantage of this is that the owner-operator can plan his own loads.

A smart phone or laptop lets you be able to view all the available loads, and the revenue paid for each load. This means you can be in control of your own business and, with practice, get loads that pay better than just mileage. What's more, it's not just about being able to select your next load; it's being able to organize a load to get you out of where you end up that puts you in control. It means that you won't be so dependent on your dispatcher getting you loads. This really makes it your trucking business and you will be more in control of where you want to run.

Since you are organizing your own loads into the future, I can see there's a good possibility you can get the good paying jobs ahead of a dispatcher who works for other drivers being paid by the mile.

The dispatcher will not be planning as far into the future as you will. You can spend more time working with the computer to get loads ahead of the dispatcher who is busy working for multiple drivers.

I think that a smart owner-operator who can work a calculator can improve his cash flow this way. It may take a few months to figure the loads out and get it right every time, but I think it would pay off in the long run. A non-driving spouse can spend time looking for loads for the driver. Your spouse can also take care of the paperwork, pay the bills and act as your public relations division as you load and unload. Sometimes the non- driving spouse does not even have to be in the truck rather they can be at home organizing loads into the future for the truck.

Independent contractors can act as trainers, with CRST Malone paying the student's wages. By being paid not by the mile but with 70 percent of the revenue that the shipper pays, you can almost double the distance you run, making it very profitable as an owner-operator. As CRST pays your student team driver's wages, you don't have the problem of hiring someone, paying them, and deducting taxes, etc.

Landstar calls its owner-operators Business Capacity Owners (BCOs) who are only paid a percentage of the revenue. Landstar likes to call their drivers "CEO's on Wheels" who choose what they want to haul and where they want to go. Their drivers are only owner-operators who own their own trucks and run their own business.

Some companies only employ owner-operators who have their own incorporated companies. I imagine this avoids the hassle of the company having to withhold things like child support payments.

For tax reasons, it pays to incorporate. I have done so as Wooderson Inc. It also helps to reduce the taxes I pay. It seems you pay social security taxes on wages but not on a dividend paid by your corporation so this is how it saves on taxes. If you are going to own your own truck, you need to seriously look at incorporating. Check with your tax advisor.

Food

You can't afford to eat three big meals a day in truck stops. It's not because of the money — it's because your health will not stand it. You'll grow fat.

Eating in truck stops is easy to do, especially when you're in a hurry. There's no waiting for your food to be cooked if you eat at a buffet. Most large truck stops have a buffet style breakfast, lunch, and dinner. With unlimited amounts of food available, I gained twenty pounds the first year — and I watched what I ate. I could have gained much more.

Walmarts are usually friendly to big rigs. If they have a grocery department, shop at Walmart. Buy fruit and vegetables you can eat raw. Buy food like rotisserie chicken, nuts and cheeses for snacks and small meals. Work out a way to only eat one meal a day at a truck stop. When eating while the truck is moving you'll drive more miles. The snacks you eat in the truck will not only keep you away from the greasy spoon restaurants but will save you time and let you run harder. Make it a point to stop and eat, fuel up, and take a shower once a day, and it won't be so hard as a team to run a thousand miles a day.

Frequent Flyer Miles

There is a perk that owner-operators can have when they pay for their fuel. Some credit cards give two frequent flyer miles for every dollar spent at a gas station. This also applies to the purchase of diesel. Hence, if an owner-operator uses a credit card that pays two points for each dollar spent then he can earn a multitude of frequent flyer miles. At times you will need to pay more for diesel if you use a credit card. But if you travel a regular route you can find diesel at a good price where credit is the same as cash. If you do end up paying more for diesel, it can be deducted for tax purposes. It seems these rewards are tax-free, so it is a good perk to have. Check with your accountant. If you have access to a discount fuel program use it. Their discounts can be quite substantial compared with double frequent flier miles.

My family members have already taken dozens of trips to Costa Rica as well as trips to New Zealand using frequent flyer miles. At one time I had enough unused miles to take over 23 trips to Costa Rica; we can visit our grandchildren at their hotel. Recently in one month the credit card I use to buy fuel gave me 98,303 miles enough miles for almost three trips to Costa Rica.

Another credit card perk is with a GM card (888-763-5655). The GM card will credit you with 5 percent of your purchase toward buying a GM vehicle. The way it works is that you negotiate the best price with your dealer on a new car purchase and then have a further $500 to $3,000 deducted (depending on the vehicle). If a new car or pickup is in your future, once you have established yourself as a truck driver this is a very good perk. Visit www.gmcard.com.

In-Cab Learning

There are many courses you can study online while on the road. The other option is to get a dedicated run and enroll in a weekend or night class at a local college.

Almost every university offers online courses, so you can fill your spare time with any type of study. Some of the study can be done as you drive when traffic is light. I've known drivers who have set up a study plan to listen to audio classes as they drive and then, when off duty not driving, to study what can't be done with audio alone.

If you study and get a degree in business management this will make you very useful to a transport company if you need to get off the road and look for a job in the transport industry.

I've known a driver who took a diesel mechanic-maintenance course while on the road. In this way, he would have a greater mechanical understanding of his tractor. He could one day work at a repair facility if he needed to give up his OTR lifestyle and find a "regular" job.

If you have found your niche in trucking and you intend to have your own small fleet use the time you have in the truck to learn about how trucks work and business management. OOIDA Online Business Education has "Education for the Professional Owner-Operator."

You can download lectures onto your phone and learn as you drive. The days of books on tape are greatly improved, you can now listen to whatever you want with the use of a smart phone. You even have plenty of time to learn another language while driving.

To be a good student it's important to understand the meaning of any new words you come across. This is easy to do in the digital age you just go to your phone and have an instant definition for every word you don't understand, but please unless you can ask Siri don't distract yourself while driving. Stop before you do the needed research, you can make a voice memo of any word and later sort out the definition. As it's good to cover new data more than once when I have worked out the definitions, I re-listen to the material again to make sure I have it and now understand it.

Most good writers and educators explain each new term they use so whatever you are studying make sure the author explains the new terms otherwise try a different author. In this book I have attempted to explain every new term I have used and added a glossary so you can look it up if needed.

How to get CDL Training

Truck-driving school can cost up to $7,000, therefore free training is a great attraction because you are being trained in a new profession at no charge. Some companies are offering ways to help drivers obtain a CDL at no cost or partial cost based on a commitment to remain with the trucking company for a certain amount of time.

When it comes to signing a driving contract, don't walk away from a contract if you wish to remain a truck driver and stay in the industry. Be aware that if you do have a contract and don't stay the required time, and don't pay what's owed, some companies will refuse to verify your employment with them when you apply for another job. This is illegal but if it happens will make it difficult for you to be hired by another company.

Here is a list of companies to get you started on your research. Information may change so keep an eye on new information online and stay in contact with the recruiter. The following companies will either train you or hire you if you have CDL from a truck-driving school.

Andrus Transportation Services
www.andrustrans.com   1 800 888 5838
Baylor Trucking
www.baylortrucking.com   1 800 322 9567 ext. 4
C. R. England Trucking
www.crengland.com   1 800 338 3634
Con-Way Truckload
www.con-way.com   1 800 CFI DRIVE
Covenant Transport
www.covenantdrivers.com   1 866 575 2308
CRST Malone
www.malonecontractors.com   1 866 513 2778
Driver Solutions
www.otrdriver.com   1 877 259 3989
FFE Transportation Services
www.ffex.net 1 800.569.9200
Marten Transport Ltd
www.martendrivingjobs.com   1 866 370 4468
Maverick Transportation
www.maverickusa.com   1 800 289 1100
May Trucking Company
www.maytrucking.com   1 800 547 9169
MCT or Midwest Coast Transport
www.mcttrans.com   1 888.310.1854
Prime Inc.
www.primeinc.com   1 877 Prime Job
Roehl Transport
www.roehl.jobs 800 535 0269

Schneider National

        www.schneiderjobs.com   1 800 44 Pride

Swift

        www.joinswift.com   1 855 279.5943

TranAm Trucking

        www.transamtruck.com 1 800 872.9609

USA Truck

        www.driveusatruck.com   1 800.684.5832

U.S. Xpress

        www.usxpress.com   1 800.879.7737

Watkins Shepard

        www.wksh.com   1 800 392.2470

Werner Enterprises

        www.werner.com   1 800.346.2818

Western Express

        www.westernexp.com   1 877 986.8855

The Future of Truck Driving

Truck Drivers in Demand

As I write this in April 2016, the future is looking remarkably good for those seeking work as OTR truck drivers. It seems to me that trucking companies cut back on personnel so much during the economic downturn that even a small increase in demand cannot be handled by existing drivers. The American Trucking Association stated in 2015 that the trucking industry was lacking 48,000 qualified drivers, which is 10,000 more than 2014, and they expect the shortage to rise to upward of 70,000 in 2016.

30-year trucking specialist, Tom McLeod, said this about truck driver shortages, "This is not a short term problem now. Many people who have been in the trucking industry for 30 years have seen driver shortages come and go. This one is not going away." The average OTR driver is 49-year-old, so 45% of all new drivers will be replacing older drivers who retire.

For the next 19 years, some 10,000 people per day will turn 65 and perhaps retire. When I go to a truck stop, I am always amazed at just how gray the workforce has become. The graying workforce is beginning to retire in large numbers. UPS expects to lose 25,000 drivers to retirement over the next five years. And as mentioned earlier, new regulations enforcing higher standards, especially for medical requirements, will take the ignition keys away from some OTR drivers.

It is well known that a recession shakes out the deadwood in the system. Companies use it as an opportunity to get rid of staff who do not perform as well as they should. As a result, many poorly performing drivers have been let go.

At the same time, many older owner-operators saw no future in replacing their trucks during the economic downturn, they got rid of their tractors and left the industry. Lack of work has encouraged other older drivers to retire. Why would they sit around a truck stop waiting for a load when retirement would allow them to spend time with their families?

And everyone was affected by the high cost of fuel during summer 2008, which crippled many independent owner-operators who couldn't pass on the fuel charges to customers; hence, they left the industry.

The 34-hour restart hours of service regulation of July 2013 has made drivers look for regional jobs where they could spend the 34 hours off with their families rather than in a truck stop with nothing to do. This is adding to the shortage of long haul drivers.

Not only has the industry lost drivers, many more drivers will be needed to transport lumber and building materials as residential construction improves. Out of work construction workers who've become truck drivers will return to their building trade that they had before the economic downturn.

With American natural gas prices at a fraction of the cost of natural gas in Europe and Japan, manufacturing will boom in America. This will cause drivers to leave the road for good paying manufacturing jobs. The increase in manufactured products will increase the demand for truck drivers.

Just like the increase in construction, it will be double whammy for trucking companies. Trucking companies will be losing drivers at a time they need the drivers most.

Solo Drivers and Teams Will Make More

Experts have predicted for years that there will need to be a substantial pay rise to attract drivers to replace retiring baby boomers.

It seems a perfect storm has been created where drivers are needed in large numbers. For years drivers have been offered other incentives such as better equipment and more home time rather than a pay raise, except team drivers pay has been raised -- they receive a five- to six-cents-per-mile increase for team driving. Trucking companies will have to bite the bullet and pay drivers much more. I think pay rates will be increased, across the industry, much sooner than anyone expected.

US Express, the 6th largest Truck load carrier, raised solo driver pay 13%, the largest increase in the company's history. Swift Transportation has also given its drivers the largest increase in pay it has ever given.

Yellow freight drivers, who are represented by the International Brotherhood of Teamsters, don't spend weeks on the road. Unlike long haul drivers, Yellow Driver drive between the YRC terminals and make it back the same night or only one day out. Yellow is now hiring drivers. They have set up their own school at their Kansas City Terminal and are working with a Teamsters' school in Indianapolis. I've mentioned earlier in the book that union jobs, because of good pay and benefits, are hard to get. But it looks like this is changing rapidly. YRC's website states, "Fully paid healthcare benefits, 401K and paid vacation time. Daily dispatches with minimum time away from home. Union contract pay rates: First year road driver can earn $60,000 and city drivers can earn $24.41/hour.

"…. Many of [YRC's] dock workers are earning CDLs or already have them and are taking additional training to qualify to drive," said Mitch Lilly, Senior Vice President of Labor and Employee Relations.

If you are desperate for work and see little or no opportunity for a job, change your mindset. Over-the-road truck drivers will still be very much in demand. It looks like the perfect storm is busting wide open the wage barrier on drivers.

If you are looking at team driving with your spouse, teams will always be in greater demand than solo drivers. To make this point in April 2016 Schneider International started offering a $15,000 sign on bonus for experienced teams. If you and your spouse are empty nesters with no money, just like we were when we started team driving, I am quite sure over the long run that trucking will be good to you and to your future financial well-being. It certainly has been for us.

You need to keep on trucking.

Warning: There is a Risk

There is a risk in hitting the road — you may never want to settle down again. Drivers talk about "diesel in the veins." It seems that once you get infected by that condition, you have to keep moving.

Writers tell stories about truckers who've had to keep moving — even to the point of leaving their families. Some truckers' wives know their husbands are not happy unless they're on the road. When my wife tells me I'm only happy when I have a truck to drive, I tell her I'm happy doing whatever I'm doing. Who knows if "diesel in your veins" is just another catchy saying with very little truth in it.

And even if having "diesel in your veins" is a condition, who says it's not a good state to be in? That is, as long as you and your spouse have the same affliction. Maybe we were naturally hunters and wanderers, and the little house on the hillside is a very recent part of our evolution.

So be warned; your whole life may change. Sunsets in Wyoming may appeal more than Facebook or Twitter. Thunderstorms in Kansas may have more impact on you than the evening news.

If "diesel in your veins" is a reality, and if it's catching and you get infected with a chronic case, I won't promise a cure but I will prescribe a treatment. When you need to rest a little more, maybe you can swap your sleeper for a little larger one — buy a diesel motor home to spend your sunset years in. You can still watch the sunrise over the desert or the stars shimmer over the canyon rim as you spend your retirement years in the wide open spaces visiting family and friends.

Ideas that May Help You

I can see truck driving being a solution for many people. If only people could look far enough into the future, they could see that after two years of OTR truck driving, they could get a job closer to home.

Empty nesters who are looking for a whole new experience should look into trucking. My wife and I discovered truck driving as empty nesters and fell in love with the freedom we gained.

I know that for most women the idea of giving up home and all the things that have been put together over a lifetime, and going away from all of this for weeks at a time in a truck, would be a huge decision. I know what it was like to get my wife's agreement to try this lifestyle. At that point we hadn't even settled in and created a home, as we had just emigrated to the U.S. from New Zealand. She finally agreed, we did it, and now she looks at this as one of the best times of her life.

I hope I have given you a good understanding how truck drivers live and work. If you do go trucking, may your life never be the same again. And may I say to you with all sincerity, just as hundreds of people have said to me and my wife almost daily, "Have a good trip."

Appendices

New Safety Era

I write this with reluctance. I've talked about truck drivers not being micromanaged that as a driver you are responsible for your actions and no one is looking over your shoulder. Well it seems that satellites in the sky can report back to your trucking company every time you move out of your lane without using a turn signal. You can get distracted or dose off and hit the ruble strip to the right or veer into the lane on the left. Mobileye®, an electronic device, will set off a buzzer and its display will show you if have moved across the white line. It will also contact head office and the driver will get a call from a real live person to check on his wellbeing. The driver will be asked if he is going to sleep and if he needs to stop to sleep.

When I first started to drive 20 years ago we didn't even have mobile phone. We had a pager to know if someone was trying to reach us. As a driver we were responsible to get the job done, no one was looking over our shoulder at our work. It was a challenging life that we responded well to.

I mentioned earlier in this book that if you need to be micromanaged get a job with a boss to tell you what to do. Now trucking has moved 180 degrees. For example, some drivers have a direct link with head office. One of my drivers while training as a team had to stay in the truck overnight. As it was a cold night they ran the engine to keep warm. This resulted in phone calls asking why the truck was idling so long.

The biggest gripe my drivers have about these new Collision Avoidance Systems (when they have rented a truck with one installed) is that the beeping goes on and on as they run through construction zones with concrete barriers that keep drivers from crossing lanes. These concrete barriers are close enough to the truck to get the buzzer going off to say the driver is too close to an object.

Also the buzzer will go off when the truck is following too close behind another vehicle. Following too close is a very bad driving fault and I don't know if my drivers have developed this bad habit or the systems in the rental trucks are overly sensitive. (To be honest, in the last few years one of my drivers did rear end another vehicle.)

My drivers have not been trained on the use of avoidance systems in the rental trucks so with better understanding of these systems, they may not have found them such a nuisance. Ted Scott, director of engineering for the American Trucking Association, said the new systems have improved in recent years. "When the systems first came on the market, there was a nuisance factor where drivers complained about false alerts." He said. "That set the technology back several years. The false target issue has diminished considerably with the new systems. Many of our companies using them are seeing some significant safety advantage."

Once again I have reluctance to admit that truck drivers because of quickly advancing technology will be micromanaged the whole time they drive. It won't even be government regulation that will put the avoidance systems on all trucks, the regulations will come from the insurance companies rather than the government. Insurance companies will see the advantage of these new systems and give substantial discounts if they are installed.

The large trucking companies that self-insure seem to have already embraced this new technology and it must be solely because they are saving money on the truck repairs, workman's comp claims and medical and physical damage to others.

In some ways this is a good trend, regulation by insurance companies with an active interest in their business is a lot better than some elected representative passing laws with no understanding of what it is about.

With the advent of electronic logging devices (ELDs) being mandatory in 2017 and the larger trucking firms using ELD's now and promising to use all electronic advances to promote safety, drivers will enter a new era of supervision. For those of you new to the industry this will be the norm and I am sure you will learn to live with it and not drive in such a way as to attract the attention of safety because you have nodded off etc.

In the long run you will be more of a professional driver because of the close supervision early in your career. It should make you a safer and happier driver and you can enjoy the freedom of the road once the rules are applied in a professional way.

Eyesight

You are in your fifties or sixties and you worry if your eyes are up to driving five to 10 years into the future. Let me tell you my story.

I was making a huge problem out of my vision. When I renewed my driver's license, the DMV official saw that my left eye was below requirements but she passed me anyway. I had just received a new prescription for glasses just to pass the test, but one eye didn't make the grade.

I had been told for years that every time I had my eyes checked, that I had cataracts. I didn't know that sometime after age 50, most of us are likely to hear our eye doctors say, "You have cataracts." Cataracts can cause blurry vision and increase the glare from lights.

I thought driving a truck may be something that belongs to my past, as I had no idea of the power of modern eye technology.

In cataract surgery, the lens inside my eyes that has become cloudy from cataract formation is removed and replaced with an artificial lens to restore clear vision. The new state of the art lens corrected my vision. The cataract surgery made such an incredible difference that the first eye received its new lens on Monday and on Thursday night, I drove to St. Louis. Before this, I was worried about driving to the grocery store.

So if you are worried about your vision and are reluctant to start a new career as an OTR truck driver, if it's just cataracts, realize that modern eye surgery is advancing at a rapid rate. By the time you need help with your sight, even my impressive results will be commonplace.

I have known Dave for 18 years. He drives for the same company as I do. He was worried about his eyes years ago, but since has had cataract surgery. He is still doing the work of a 40-year-old

155

even though he is now 75 years old.

Today, cataract surgery is one of the most routine operations performed in the United States. It is one of the safest and most effective types of surgery. About 90 percent of patients have better vision after the surgery. It takes about 15 minutes but the nurses tell me that my doctor, Dr. Fang, is so efficient he usually does it in about 12 minutes.

Thank you, Doctor Fang, I have my life back.

Extra Types of Pay

Here are some of the extra items you may be paid for in addition to miles driven.

* Payments are made for detention or Layover Pay: these are times you have no work
    * Breakdown Pay: when you can't work
    * Loading and Unloading Pay
    * Some companies even pay Congestion Pay if you deliver in New York
    * Stop Pay: some companies pay for each stop, or each stop after the first
    * Local work can be paid for by the hour
    * Tarp Pay is when you get paid for your time when you cover the load with a tarpaulin
    * Walkboard Pay is when there's no loading dock to back into and you have to use a long ramp (or walkboard) to unload. You walk up and down the walkboard as you load or unload. A walkboard is also used to load or unload household furniture at the customer's home.
    * You can get extra if you use a hand-propelled jack to load or unload
    * Some companies pay extra for hazardous material loads, called Hazmat. If both team drivers have a Hazmat Endorsement, there can be extra pay even when not carrying Hazmat loads.

* A Productivity Bonus can be paid for miles run over a certain figure each month, like 10,000 miles for a solo or 20,000 miles for a team.

Unigroup – The Best Company I've Ever Worked For

Driver Ed has been contracted to Mayflower Transit the household moving company since 1994. He and his co-driver Cherry started out working the truck load electronics division of Mayflower. Electronics includes copiers, medical equipment and freight that needed extra care like pad wrapping and strapping it firmly to the trailer wall.

Mayflower is now part of Unigroup which is formed by two van lines both involved in moving household furniture and electronics composed of United Van Lines and Mayflower Transit.

In 1998 Ed and Cherry were offered a dedicated route between Los Angeles and St Louis. This involved less than truckload (LTL) and now carry up to 30 different orders composed mainly of electronics. He now has two trucks driven by teams and another five trucks driven by solo drivers for a total of seven trucks.

Mayflower and United use independent franchise agents who own their own warehouses and smaller delivery trucks. Unigroup now seems an opportunity to expand their LTL fleet into general freight as well as electronics. Hubs are to be set up on existing agents premises and the existing agents can use their straight truck to deliver to the final destination. As Unigroup does not own OTR trucks they contract with owner-operators and Driver Ed will be in a position to get more contracts and employ more drivers.

Unigroup management under the guidance of Edward Danzer envisions rapid growth of their less than truck load fleet. All the physical infrastructure in the form of warehouses and straight trucks as controlled by their agents are in place, now they are building electronic infrastructure. Scanners will need to scan in every piece of freight. A web site is being created so you can get a quote to move a piano, or even a Harley Davidson motorcycle delivered to your living room or garage. So readers if you want something shipped in the future check out the rates and speed of delivery of **unigroup.com**.

Edward Danzer envisions another 350 OTR trucks will be needed as the LTL fleet starts servicing the multiple hubs established across America. If you are a current owner operator looking for a dedicated run call Phil to apply (Phone 636-305-4740).

I've been with Mayflower for over 20 years and they have always treated me right with friendly helpful people to name a few, Jackie, Barb, Frank, Kristi and Edward takes interest in his drivers. The pay her mile is good I have never found anything that compares and the fuel surcharge is higher than most.

If you are an owner operator with your own truck or fleet let Phil know where you want to run and ask to be emailed if something comes up that may work for you.

Good Health is Possible

In trucking sitting too long can be a problem but modern technology is here to help. It is suggested by experts that a body must take 5000 steps a day to maintain health. 10,000 steps are needed to lose weight. With 1760 yards in a mile it means we need to move 5 to 6 miles a day if we are overweight. Smart watches are designed to keep track of the number of steps taken each day. My Fitbit also shows the heart beats per minute miles walked, calories needed and number of floors climbed.

Now that by law, a driver has to take a 30-minute break if he works longer than 8 hours you have the opportunity to stretch your legs and walk. Every time you stop the truck check with your watch how many steps you go to walk around your rig as you eyeball the tires etc. Walk around the truck a few times it's about 60 steps when you stop to stretch your legs. So five times is 300 steps. If a fast walk is about 4mph so you need to walk for one and a half hours a day. Some of these steps are part of your regular schedule so you might be surprised that if you spend your half hour break walking it will be a small burden to get to the 10,000 steps each day.

The health benefit will make it all worthwhile. Joseph has been sticking to doing 10,000 steps and has lost 80lb. I was walking past a neighbor and he asked after my walk. I looked at my watch and said so far today I've done 5560 steps, he pulled out his device and said he had already hit 5500 steps. So let's get truck drivers walking showing each driver you meet, how many steps you have done, and see how long it is before they respond to you with the steps they have done.

I have already mentioned the X-iser, my small compact treadmill. I had one of these small steppers in the sleeper and I used to exercise while my wife drove. She got so tired of tripping over it I got rid of it. This new X-iser folds flat enough to slip under the lower bunk. So on those very hot or cold days you can take your steps in the tractor. You can also exercise as the truck moves if you drive as a team.

You don't have to be in a truck to get the benefits of an X-iser. I built a desk in my office so I can stand up as I work, I made it high enough so I can stand on the X-iser. To keep my body active and moving I use the X-iser when standing and slowly move my legs up and down as I work. I find I can do this without distracting my attention from the work I'm doing. When I need to unfix my attention I do a sudden burst as explained in the owner's exercise manual. "It is an "all out" effort, a sprint of not more than 60 seconds."

The X-iser is a quality built machine available from the manufacturer. Mention I sent you and I will be sent a check for $50. Good for me but super good for you, you can direct all the drivers you meet to get their steps in with an X-iser and make fifty bucks each time.

My early years were spent milking cows in New Zealand. As a farmer I understood the importance of minerals for good animal health so when I came across marine phytoplankton (microscopic ocean plants). I realized this was how to get all the nutrients the body so badly needs.

Oceans Alive marine phytoplankton contains the full-spectrum of nutrients your body needs at a cellular level which provides an increase in energy that builds up significantly when it is ingested on a daily basis.

What impressed me the most about taking Oceans Alive was the instant boost of mental energy with no downside (not like a sugar high). I feel this is so important for truck drivers I just had to include it in this book. Do your own research on Oceans Alive and try it yourself.

It seems too good to be true that a dropper full of Oceans Alive can revitalize the body in moments and keep you safe on the road.

Knuckles our dog only needs one drop of Oceans Alive to keep him very active. When he is in the car he is "on duty, not driving" always taking in what is happening around him.

Glossary

1st seat driver — The most experienced driver who is in charge.

2nd seat driver — The second driver, who can be someone in training.

18 wheeler — Tractor and one or two trailers with a total of 18 wheels. Also known as a big rig or semi.

401(k) plan — A program where the company pays in money for your retirement. You can also pay in money. The money you pay in is not taxable.

80,000 lbs. — The maximum weight a truck can carry with one or two trailers. About 26,000 kilos, 40 short tons American weight, or almost 36 long tons British weight.

9 to 5 — 9 a.m. to 5 p.m., the regular hours for most people who work in an office.

AC adapter — It allows electrical equipment that is usually run by a battery to be plugged into a wall plug of a home or hotel room.

Aerodynamics — The study of how gasses move around solid bodies such as aircrafts, trucks and cars.

Agency — The office and warehouse that household goods carriers have in most cities.

Agent — Someone who represents a trucking company. Agents obtain loads.

Air bag — A bag made from very tough material that air is pumped into under pressure. It supports the load and smooths out the ride.

Air brakes — Compressed air, supplied by a compressor to work the brakes in a truck.

Air ride — When a tractor's or trailer's suspension is supported by air bags. It gives a rig a smoother ride.

Air ride cab — The driver's cab in a tractor that is supported by air bags to smooth out the ride.

Air seat — An air-supported seat that gives a smoother ride.

Air suspension — When compressed air bags are used to smooth out a truck's ride, as opposed to steel springs.

Articulate — Refers to the ability to move or bend, as a tractor and trailer does.

Automatic transmission — A transmission that shifts gears by itself.

Axles — The shaft or rod that goes between the wheels.

Baby boomers — The generation of people who were born after World War II.

Backhaul — Return trip. It is when you haul a load back.

Base plate — Another word for the truck registration plate.

Bells and whistles — All the fancy extras.

Benefits — Job benefits can include health insurance, life insurance, bonuses.

Big rig — A term only used in the United States to denote a tractor and trailer. Also known as an 18 wheeler or semi. In England, it is known as an articulated truck. Shortened to "Artic."

Blanket wrap — See Pads.

Bobtail — When you drive a truck without a trailer, like a cat without a tail.

Book miles — A computer program made for household goods movers that tells the shortest mileage between two places. The program does not follow the interstate freeways and in many cases does not show all of the miles a truck needs to run.

Booking agents — See Agents.

Bottom Line — A bookkeeping term meaning how much money is left at the end, or, on the bottom line on the balance sheet.

Break (take a) — Have a rest or make a change.

Brokers — Brokers earn a commission by getting work from firms needing goods transported, and finding trucks or transport firms to ship the goods.

Bulk carriers — Tank trailers that carry liquid.

Cab-over — The truck has no hood because the driver sits over the motor.

Cargo — The goods that trucks, trains, planes and ships haul.

Carrier — A company that moves freight or carries people. In this sense, a trucking firm.

CB radio — Short for Citizens' Band Radio. Two-way radios that allow people within close range to talk to each other.

CDL Class A — A Commercial Driver's License. Class A means that a driver can drive a big rig.

Chains — Steel wires or chains placed over tires to grip on ice or snow.

Check his mirrors — Look in side-view mirrors to see what's coming up behind him.

Claim — When freight is damaged, a claim is made to cover the cost.

Clutch — With a stick shift transmission, the clutch engages or disengages the engine from the drive train.

Combination Vehicle — One that articulates. Its joined sections can move separately from each other.

Company — In this book, the term refers to a firm that moves freight.

Company driver — Drivers working for wages or paid by the mile who don't own their own tractors. The company owns the tractors.

Company-Owned Truck — The company owns the tractor. The driver is a company driver.

Compression — The compression of an engine is measured by the amount of pressure built up as the piston compresses the air in the cylinder just before the fuel is ignited. This force is also used to slow a vehicle down when the foot is off the gas pedal and no fuel is being burned. This is why a truck has to shift to a lower gear before it goes down a steep grade.

Compressor — A pump that puts air under pressure.

Concrete (set in...) — A condition, usually legal or budgetary, that is unable to be changed or moved.

Containerized shipping — Cargo containers that are moved by ships, trains, or trucks.

Coolant — The water in the radiator and engine block. Special chemicals are added and then the water is known as coolant.

Conventional — A truck just like most cars, with a motor in front of the driver. The truck has a hood — sometimes conventionals are known as hoods.

Couple — Two people who are married or in a relationship (a partner), a common type of driving team.

Custom-built — Made to order. No two custom-built sleepers are exactly the same; each one is designed to fit the owner's needs.

Cylinders — Most modern truck engines have six cylinders. The chamber in the engine is where the fuel is burned and the pistons are pushed down to produce power.

Dead head — Running a tractor and trailer with no load. It's "dead" running, no one is paying for the truck to "head" out and pick up a load in another city.

Dedicated route — A route that a truck follows on a regular basis. Also called a dedicated run. It allows the driver regular time at home. It is one of the best trucking jobs available.

Depots — Places from which transport companies operate.

Diesel #2 — Number-two grade diesel is the diesel fuel used except in extreme cold. Then number one diesel is used. Diesel has more oil in it than gasoline, and will not catch fire or explode as easily. All over-the-road trucks run on diesel.

Differential — When a vehicle travels around a corner the outer driving wheel must turn faster than the inner driving wheel. This is achieved with the use of a differential. It is a large round casing between the rear wheels that the drive shaft goes into.

Dispatch — The office of a trucking company that coordinates freight pick-up and delivery.

Dispatcher — The person in the company the driver works with to get loads and keep moving. Can also be called the Fleet Manager.

D.O.T (the) — The Department of Transportation, a federal agency that regulates transport. Some states also have their own D.O.T.

Dolly — A dolly is a type of small trailer that supports a semi-trailer when coupled to a truck.

Double clutching — A driving technique used in trucks without a synchromesh transmission. The clutch is put in, and the gear shift is moved to neutral. The clutch is put in again and the gear shift is moved to another gear. Since the clutch has to be put in twice, it's called double clutching.

Doubles — A tractor pulling two trailers.

Down payment — The amount of money you must pay at the beginning if you buy something that you need to borrow money to pay for. Down payments are usually for costly items like homes, cars and trucks.

Driver advocate — Some firms have an advocate to look after the drivers' welfare separately from the dispatchers. The person who makes sure that the drivers' pay is correctly handled.

Driver turnover — Some companies have a driver turnover rate as high as 300 percent, which means in theory that three times a year all of the drivers are replaced. In practice, it means that while many long-term drivers will stay for years, a lot of recently hired drivers will leave after a few weeks.

Drop and hook — Where one trailer is dropped and the driver hooks on to another, already loaded trailer.

Drug and alcohol testing — Before a driver can be employed he must pass a drug test. A driver can be asked to take a drug and alcohol test at any time.

Dual wheels — Two wheels together on the same side of the axle.

DUI or DWI — Driving Under the Influence, or Driving While Intoxicated. Driving with too much alcohol or drugs in your body.

E-mail — Sending messages via the Internet.

Eating out — Eating in restaurants, truck stops, fast food places, etc.

Education debt — The money someone owes to pay for his/her education.

Electronics — High value items like computers, copiers and medical scanners, etc.

Endorsement — It is something that is added to your driver's license to enable you to legally drive vehicles other than cars. Like buses or big rigs. An endorsement is also needed to haul hazardous material known as Hazmat.

En route — On the way.

Empty nesters — Parents whose children have left home.

Engine block — The main part of the engine that contains the cylinders where the fuel burns. Coolant flows through the engine block to take the heat to the radiator to be dispersed.

Equipment — The tractors and trailers necessary to move goods.

Exhaust manifold — The place where the burned gasses leave the engine.

Exhibit house — A company that builds the booths you see at fairs and trade shows.

Exit numbers — A number given to a freeway exit. Sometimes, especially in Western states, the exit number will be the same as the mile marker. This makes it very easy to know how far you need to go. If the exit is 190 and you are at mile marker 90 you have 100 miles to go in the state. Other states may have exit numbers going one, two, three, etc.; if they put in a new exit it is usually named with a B. Exit 2B, for example. This system is not as workable as having the exit numbers match the mile marker numbers. Exit numbers are on up to date maps and should be used to know when to leave the freeway.

Facilities — The restrooms, shower rooms, food servicing areas, phones, etc., at a truck stop.

Fail (brakes will) — In the case of brakes, too much heat will cause them to stop working, or fail.

Fast food outlets — Chain eateries like McDonald's, Burger King, Taco Bell, etc.

Fast lane — The outside (leftmost) lane on the highway, used for running fast or passing. Life in the Fast Lane means that things are moving fast.

Felony — A crime that is punished by death or a prison term longer than a year.

Fifth wheel — Fifth wheel originally meant the area on a horse-drawn carriage that supported the front axle and allowed the carriage to steer. Now it is used to mean the wheel-shaped device that the trailer sits on over the rear axle(s) of the tractor and allows the rig to bend in the middle when going around corners. Fifth wheel is also the name of a recreational trailer that is attached to a pickup truck that is fitted with a fifth wheel.

Flat bed — An open trailer for carrying machinery and things too large or awkward to fit inside a van type body.

Fleet — A number of vehicles under one ownership.

Fleet Operator— Someone who owns more than one truck.

Forced dispatch — When the driver has no choice of which loads to take and must take all loads the dispatcher books for him.

Forklift — A moveable machine with two prongs that stick out in front that can raise or lower to load or unload trucks.

Friction point — The point where the clutch begins to bite, and the vehicle begins to move as you let out the clutch.

Fuel desk — The place at a truck stop where you pay for your diesel.

Fuel injection — A device that injects a measured amount of fuel into the cylinders of the engine.

Fuel saving bonus — A sum of money paid to the driver for driving correctly and saving fuel.

Fuel surcharge — Extra money charged to the shipper to cover excessive fuel costs. As a result, extra money is paid to the owner-operator as a fuel surcharge.

Gelling — Diesel fuel contains wax. In very cold weather, the wax solidifies (known as gelling). The engine stops running because the diesel will not flow. Trucks that run in very cold weather have heaters in the fuel tanks to stop the diesel from gelling.

General dry goods — Most goods that get carried in a van-type trailer.

Generator — A device for producing electricity.

Goods — Things trucks transport.

Governor — A device that prevents a vehicle from exceeding a pre-set speed.

Grade — When highways are made evenly sloping, signs will be posted when going downhill stating the percentage of the grade. On a 4 percent grade, you drop 4 feet for every 100 feet you travel. Truck drivers must respond to these signs by changing down to a lower gear and reducing speed.

Graduation bonus — Sum of money paid to a new driver once he has completed the company's training program.

Grapevine — A windy mountain pass north of Los Angeles on the I-5 freeway.

Guarantee — A promise. If a company guarantees you $500 a week, you should be paid this, even if you don't run any miles.

Hassle — A problem.

Haul — To move, to carry, to transport.

Hauling produce — Moving fruits and vegetables

Hazmat — Hazardous materials that require special handling.

Inter-axle differential — This is controlled by the driver of a tandem-axle truck. A switch on the dashboard will be labeled "lock-unlock." This enables the power from the engines to be transferred equally to both axles to gain more traction, and as a result the truck doesn't get stuck with one-wheel spinning.

Intermodal — Involving two or more different modes of transportation to move cargo.

Interstate — Multi-lane divided roads that connect major cities. Interstate signs are blue with white numbers. Interstate refers to between states. This is different than intrastate, which means within the borders of that state.

Intrastate — Within the boarder of a single state as different from interstate which is between more than one state.

Inventory — A detailed list of articles being shipped. In moving household goods, an inventory is needed that documents any previous marks or scratches.

Irregular route carrier — Carriers who move loads to any destination. They do not operate on regular schedules.

Jack knife — Means to double up like a foldable pocket knife. In trucking, this means the tractor and trailer folded up together, the trailer having caught up to the tractor in an accident. To jack knife a trailer into a loading dock means that the tractor will be at an angle to the trailer.

Jake brake — An engine compression brake. Also known as an engine retarder.

Labor — People needed to do a job.

Layover — When you stop and take a day or more off.

Layover allowance or pay — A small sum of money the driver gets for being stuck in some place without work.

Leaf spring — A spring for vehicles made of curved steel strips. The front spring on any large truck is a leaf spring.

Learner's license — Just like driving a car, you must pass a written test before you learn to drive a big rig.

Legible — Easy to read.

Less than truck load — LTL. Some carriers carry many small loads from different shippers. This is known as LTL.

Life insurance — Insurance that pays a pre-determined amount of money on death. Some companies provide this at no charge to the driver. It may only cover accidental death.

Light weight — The weight of an empty truck.

Livestock — Live animals like pigs and cows.

Logistics — The calculating of every element (driver, vehicle, fuel, route, etc.) needed to move a load from here to there.

Loading bay — A place where a truck backs in to load or unload. Can also be called a loading dock.

Loads — Usually OTR drivers take full loads from one place to another. LTL firms operate trucks that pick up and drop off loads in different places.

Log book — A driver has to record the hours he is on duty in a paper book or electronic logging device.

Log book violations — Not following the hours of service regulations.

Lumbar support — The support that is needed in the center of the back to keep the curve in the spine.

Lumpers — Workers who unload and load trucks by hand.

Machine tools — Expensive machines that work with little or no direction. Machine tools perform the heavy grinding and cutting chores in metalworking shops.

Mile marker — A sign on the side of the road telling the distance to (or from) the state line or the end of the freeway.

Mileage basis — The way most drivers are usually paid. Pay for the miles run, with no overtime pay.

Miles per gallon (mpg) — The number of miles a vehicle can travel on one gallon of fuel.

Millennial — Generational name for people born between the early 80s and the early 2000s.

Motel layover — When a transport firm advertises motel layover, it means that they will pay for the motel when you stop and take a day or more off.

Name of the game — Slang; meaning what it's all about.

Neutral — When the transmission shift is not in forward or reverse gear, it is in neutral.

Non-forced dispatch — The driver has the right to turn any load down, without reason.

Non-union — A job with no union to negotiate wages and conditions.

NOx — See Oxides of Nitrogen below.

Odometer — A device in the center of the speedometer that records the total mileage that the vehicle has traveled.

Off-duty time — The time shown in a log book when the driver is relieved of all work duties and is not responsible for the truck.

OOIDA — Owner-Operators Independent Drivers Association are a drivers' advocacy group that fights for the rights of all drivers as well as providing news, education and services for truck drivers.

On-duty time — When a driver is driving, loading, etc.

On duty, not driving — The hours a driver spends fueling and inspecting, loading or supervising the loading and unloading of his truck.

Operations — The department of a carrier that organizes loads, dispatches trucks and handles customers.

Orientation — A period of training when the new driver learns the policies of the transport company he is joining. For an experienced driver, this doesn't take long.

OTR — Over-the-Road. When you drive a truck and don't get home every night. You can be out as long as 6-8 weeks before you get home.

Oxides of Nitrogen (NOx) — Nitrogen oxides are exhaust elements that contribute to the formation of smog, acid rain and greenhouse gas levels. The high temperature at which diesel combustion occurs produces NOx. The hotter the combustion, the more NOx is created.

Out — In trucking terms it means away from home. "I've been out for six weeks."

Out-of-state license — You can train in another state. You transfer your license to the state you are training in and get a learner's permit. This is a simple, established procedure.

Owner-operator — When a driver owns his own tractor and possibly the trailer.

P&D driver — Local pick-up and delivery driver.

Pads — The blankets that household furniture gets wrapped in to protect it while it's being moved. The terms "blanket" or "blanket-wrap" are also used.

Pay package — The complete package of payment, which may include bonuses or a health plan, etc.

Per diem — Latin for Per Day. Meaning a tax-free sum of money, a driver is entitled to each day for eating out, because he is away from home and can't cook his own meals.

Per mile — Each mile. If you were paid 40 cents each mile, for driving 600 miles in a day you would receive $240.

Percent of the money — Some companies pay a driver a percent of the money the carrier gets for transporting a load. Owner-operators more commonly work on a percentage of the load.

Permits — Authority from a state to run a big rig on their roads.

Placards — Signs. The Hazmat placard is in the shape of a diamond.

Planners — Company staff who plan how loads are moved.

Practical miles — Practical miles is when you are paid using measurements based on actual addresses or zip codes, and use common-sense routing, even if going by the interstate is longer.

Predictable schedule — When you know where you will be in the future.

Preferential treatment — Receiving favors or giving preference. Some companies will give first choice of loads to team drivers ahead of solo drivers.

Produce — Fruits and vegetables.

Public scales — A set of scales that the public can use. Anyone who pays the required fee can weigh their truck.

Radiator — Part of the cooling system that removes heat from the coolant passing through it.

Recruiter — The person of the company responsible for hiring new drivers or owner-operators.

Reefer — A refrigerated trailer used to carry temperature-sensitive loads.

Referral bonus — Payment to a driver who encouraged another driver to join his company.

Regional — Operating only in a specific area of the country.

Registration — Having a vehicle registered with the state and paying the fees involved.

Revs — The number of revolutions per minute the engine is turning over. All trucks have rev counters to show this.

Rig — A horse and carriage was sometimes called a rig. Now, when we talk of a big rig, we usually mean a tractor-trailer combination.

RV — Recreational vehicle. A motor home or travel trailer. Travel trailers are connected to the tow vehicle in different ways. A regular travel trailer is connected to a car, SUV or pickup with a bumper level ball hitch. A fifth wheel travel trailer can only to towed by a pickup because it is attached to the vehicle with a specialized bed mounted hitch called a fifth wheel. Just the same way a big rigs trailer is attached.

RV park — Recreational vehicle parks are where motor homes and trailers can park and connect up to electricity and water. Vacationers can stay overnight or longer.

Safety violation — When a truck has a fault that could make it unsafe.

Satellite Navigation System (SNS) — A computer-based system that gets its position from satellites so the company knows exactly where the truck is.

Scanner — An electronic device that scans to see if radar is being used.

Semi (slang) — A tractor-trailer combination.

Service bay — An area where a vehicle is worked on or serviced.

Shop fittings — The shelves and counters where goods are displayed in a shop.

Short miles — Sometimes known as book miles or household goods miles. When the computer routes you via the shortest distance, without taking the interstate route into account.

Sign-on bonus — A sum of money paid to an experienced driver to start working for a transport company. The bonus is not usually paid all at once but can be spread over a year and paid quarterly.

Single driver — Only one driver at a time. Can also be called a solo driver. Until recently this is how trucks were operated. Now two drivers can team up and one sleeps while the other drives.

Sleepers — Also known as sleeper berths. The area behind the driver and passenger seats where a bed or beds are provided for the driver to sleep. On the road the driver lives in the truck.

Slip seating — When a driver does not have exclusive use of a truck. The term is used because one driver slips out of a seat and the other driver slips into it. For OTR drivers, you drive a different truck every time you go to work.

Spec or specked — Short for specification. If a truck was specked for mountain driving it would include a Jake Brake.

Specialized carrier — A carrier that only transports a particular type of freight. Car-hauling, livestock, and trade shows are all examples of specialized carriers.

Specific lanes — When a company runs OTR, but is back and forth between two separate areas.

Split speed limits — Where cars have a higher speed limit than trucks.

Spouse rider program — Allows the wife or husband of the driver, or partner, to accompany the driver on a trip.

Straight truck — A truck that includes the engine and cargo area all on one chassis. Different from a semi that has the cargo in a separate trailer.

Synchromesh — A device in an automobile with a stick shift transmission that regulates the speed of the gears so they can mesh together without grinding when shifting gears.

Tandem axle — A three axle truck with two rear axles. These are known as tandem axles.

Tankers — A large tank built into a trailer for moving liquids, also known as bulk delivery.

Tarp — A tarpaulin cover for an open top trailer.

Tarp pay — Extra pay for a driver who spends time covering a load on a flatbed trailer with a tarpaulin.

Tax advantage — Means that you pay less tax, or the tax that you pay is deferred into the future.

Team — Two people who share the same truck and take turns driving. One drives while the other sleeps. Often it is husband and wife, but it can be father and son, or people who have no relationship. A team is paid more per mile than a single driver.

Team operation — When a truck is operated by two drivers.

Teamsters union — A union involved in the trucking industry.

Union members are paid on an hourly basis with overtime. Experience is needed and there is no shortage of drivers for these jobs, as the pay is good.

Torque — A twisting force that is used to turn the drive shaft and move a vehicle forward.

Tractor — The unit used to tow a trailer. A tractor can have two axles and six wheels, or three axles and ten wheels.

Trade — A type of work requiring specific skills such as plumbing, carpentry or roofing.

Trade qualification — A certificate to show that you have studied and trained in a line of work that requires specific skills and tools.

Trainer — An experienced driver who teams with a student who has completed truck school and has a CDL. To start with, the trainer watches from the passenger seat and corrects all of the student's driving faults. Once the trainer is confident that the student is capable of handling the truck on the freeway, they can team drive. The trainer will then spend some weeks with the student to build his confidence and to teach him how to handle any situation that may arise. The end result, if the trainer has done a good job, is a very safe driver who will be able to handle any situation.

Transmission — The part of the vehicle that sends power to the driving axle. It contains sets of gears that allow the vehicle to run at different speeds.

Transport company — A firm that moves freight.

Trip — A journey, or run, that someone makes between two places; in this context, a truck driver.

Trip number — The number a company gives to each trip to keep track of payment owed to a driver.

Triples — Three trailers (legal in some states).

Truck driving school — A place where you learn to drive an 18-wheeler big rig.

Truck stop facilities — The restroom, shower rooms, food service area, phones or other amenities at truck stops.

Truckie — Slang for a truck driver.

Turbocharger — A rotor spun by the exhaust gasses that compresses air before it goes into the cylinders.

UPS — United Parcel Service.

Under contract — When a written agreement exists.

Union drivers — Drivers with a union to negotiate their wages and working conditions.

Valve — A tap that controls the flow of liquid or gas through a pipe, or out of an enclosed space, by opening and closing.

Van lines — This usually refers to a household goods company that moves household furniture.

Van type — A trailer that is enclosed.

Write the business — Means to get the business. Usually when business is obtained, a contract is written, hence, "write the business."

Yard Jockey – a purpose built tractor designed to move trailers into loading docks in a third the time it takes an OTR tractor

Made in the USA
Monee, IL
29 June 2022

98803385R10105